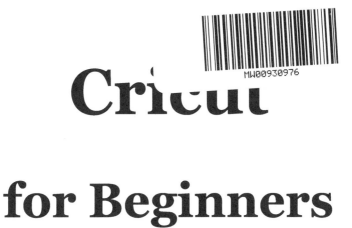

Cricut

for Beginners

The Complete Guide to Start From Zero to Master Any Cricut Machine, Tools, and Materials. Tips and Tricks with Many Project Ideas Included

By

Sharon Cope

The information herein is offered for informational purposes solely and is universal as so. The presentation of the information is without a contract or any type of guarantee assurance.

The trademarks that are used are without any consent, and the publication of the trademark is without permission or backing by the trademark owner. All trademarks and brands within this book are for clarifying purposes only and are owned by the owners themselves, not affiliated with this document.

Table of Contents

Introduction

Cricut's inception in 2006 by Provo Craft & Novelty, Inc, Cricut has experienced a number of iterations and improvements. The company's die-cutting machine has been so popular among craftsmen that it has spawned many iterations. The Cricut has always given artists a wide range of options for producing high-quality works that can be sold for a profit. Whether there is a Cricut veteran or just starting out, It is probably seen in the wide variety of products sold at craft fairs and niche shops, from popular sayings and quotations stenciled on wood signs to personalized water tumblers.

In the hands of a Cricut expert, vinyl lettering may mimic the appearance of hand-painted signs. Vinyl letters so securely adhere to one another that it would be impossible to remove any of them by hand. That's how lifelike it can be made to seem. The majority of types of vinyl also retain their durability in wet environments. This opens a world of possibilities for creating fantastic items for both the inside and outside of the home. Despite the continued popularity of scrapbooking, It may be seen a decline in the availability of scrapbooking supplies like sticker sheets and even whole scrapbooking sections at certain shops due to the proliferation of the Cricut. This is not mean that one cannot have fun with scrapbooking; on the contrary, the possibilities are almost limitless. Many Cricut versions now have Bluetooth connectivity for simple device pairing and wireless data transfer. The compact size of a Cricut machine is one of its many advantages. It's approximately as big as a home printer, but there is a need for a lot of room to spread out the supplies. All the magic that occurs before the projects are cut with a Cricut happens outside of the actual structural space. Not only may it be used and transferred for textual styles and images in this area, but it can also be used for high-quality Cricut images and text styles through separate purchases like Cricut Access and Cartridges. Designed and manufactured by Provo Craft, Cricut has been a best-seller for quite some time. As more and more people explore the world of modern craftsmanship and makeovers, many people have forgotten about scrapbooking and paper designs. The Cricut shaper machine is perhaps the most popular Cricut product. Any hard-working specialist may create new forms and designs by inserting a cartridge into the shaper.

Given its amazing guidance in the realm of planning, many individuals save heavily for this device. Some people like the Cricut Expression series, which is great for those who want to go into more complex topics like silk screening and the use of vinyl and card stock in their creations. Each machine is also capable of using Cricut-made cartridges to design custom patterns and looks. A copy of the Cricut Design Studio package, which is required in order to link a Cricut slicing machine to a computer if anyone wants to learn more and more about using the machine through the PC. All of the images from the Cricut cartridge collection are included in this offering. It's common knowledge among crafters and scrapbookers that the Cricut cutting machine, when loaded with a suitable structural cartridge, is an excellent way to create precise cuts for a wide variety of unique projects. What it accomplished was more than only spark originality and skill; it also made scrapbooking easy and accessible to anybody. Actually, today even those who lack the skills to do so will be able to create their artwork. There is no requirement for astounding attractive items or enchanting strategies while producing Christmas upgrades or Christmas cards. The Christmas Cricut Cartridge eliminates the need for scissors. The Cricut cartridge and a few tips may serve as inspiration. And with Cricut, the possibilities are endless.

Chapter 01: Familiarity With Design Space

In order to get the most out of your Cricut machine, you need to become acquainted with Cricut Design Space, the company's official online platform. That's not programming, by the way; it's something that can be downloaded as a module to a computer or an app to a tablet or smartphone and then customized. Designs and images imported from outside of Design Space may now be used with it. The downloadable Cricut Design Space software is costless. While it's true that everyone should keep a log, Cricut Design Space is a web-based coding environment that lets you connect your cutting machines wirelessly or through USB. It's how you produce all the cool stuff that gets printed on things like t-shirts, pillows, coffee mugs, and more. Instead of producing or downloading the designs from Cricut, you can just scan the items you need, look for them using the keyword SVG in the search bar towards the bottom of any Etsy page, and then "play" with the designs.

There are some free images and text styles included in the application, but there are also others that cost money. A Cricut Access Plan may also be pursued, providing access to a library of images and fonts for use with the machine. However, information may be downloaded in a variety of text formats to the computer, and photographs can be uploaded to Design Space that anybody has created, discovered for free, or otherwise acquired independently. It doesn't need to install anything on the computer to use Cricut Design

Space since it's web-based. Some modules, however, need to be downloaded; this prompt should appear automatically and be short when encountering the underlying operation. The job may then be seen on any authorized device. However, when working with an iPhone or iPad, there is an option to keep it contained to the device itself. The Cloud, though, should almost always be the first suggestion. It's possible to use Design Space on Mac, PC, and iOS devices.

Chromebooks are ineligible since they use Google's Chrome OS rather than Windows or Mac OS. A tangle on a page may sometimes prevent cutting the design and replace it with a message informing that payment is required. It may go back to the canvas and check each photo to see whether there is a dollar sign underneath it or if the text style you selected has a dollar symbol. Keep in mind that you still do not have access to ALL the images and text styles even if you have Cricut Access. Projects selected from Design Space may have used a premium image or font style at your expense. The task's instructions should include whether or not you have to pay to participate. Sometimes they'll send out an email warning of an impending power outage. In practice, though, I find that this is seldom the case. Cricut Design Space's cutting feature is one of my favorite features. It is really a likable feature eliminating the many fonts, colors, and patterns from text and images. Even yet, there will be times when it fails. Here are a few ideas to consider if anybody finds this to be an issue:

Check that the image or text style you want to delete (which is superimposed on another image) is included entirely inside the target image. If any of it is protruding, it will not be effective. Verify your selections thoroughly.

Remember that there are two layers to remove from the image when you cut it: the first, the picture/text style that you sliced, and the second, the actual cut.

1.1 Print and Cut option

Due to the sheer size of "Print and Cut," It will be delving into it too much. However, in the experience, the most common reason why people are having trouble with "Print and Cut" is because it does not smooth their photographs. Make sure "Select All" and "Straighten" are pressed before going to "Print and Cut." When trying to launch Cricut Design Space, nothing happens. Errors or a blank screen might appear while using Design Space if it does not have the most recently updated module. If the page is blank, then one may try refreshing it to see if the module update appears. Leave this page while it is refreshing, and find that it has gone completely white.

1.2 Cartridge

Parts stored in cartridges are used to create cartridge designs. Every single cartridge comes with its own console overlay and manual. Important decisions for the cartridge are shown on the plastic console overlay.

But Provo Craft has just released an "All-inclusive Overlay" that works with all cartridges released after August 1, 2013. The idea behind the universal overlay is to make slicing easier by requiring the player to memorize just one console overlay as opposed to the overlays for each unique cartridge. Cricut Design Studio package on a personal computer, a USB-connected Gypsy machine, or the console overlay on the Cricut mechanism itself may all be used to delete designs. Cartridges may be divided into two categories based on their physical appearance and the language used in their labels.

One cartridge may be used for a number of various cuts thanks to its array of unique features. More than 275 cartridges with textual styles and forms are already available (decoupled from the machine), and more are added every month. There are some standard-issue cartridges, but Cricut also has licensing agreements with companies like Disney, Pixar, NBC, Sesame Workshop, DC Comics, and Hello Kitty. Although there is a wide price range in the Cricut line, all cartridges are compatible, even if not all of the features on a given cartridge are usable on the smaller machines. All cartridges can only be used with Cricut software, are bound to a single user, and cannot be transferred or resold. When the machine is turned off, the cartridge that was purchased for it is likely to be useless. Because Cricut has the right to discontinue support for older versions of their product at any time, certain cartridges may become obsolete quite rapidly. The 'Cricut Craft Room software allows users to combine images from many cartridges, merge images, besides stretch/turn images, but it does not permit the creation of user-defined patterns. Further, it allows the customer to see the finished product through on-screen images before initiating the cutting process. Cricut announced on July 15 that the Cricut Craft Room would be closing due to Adobe's abandonment of Flash. Customers owning "legacy" equipment were given a discount to upgrade to machines compatible with the Cricut Design Space. As of July 16, 2018, 'Design Space' is the primary software that may be used to create projects. Cartridges purchased before the Cricut Mini's October 2018 power cut are not fully compatible with Design Space.

1.3 Third-Party

In practice, Provo Craft has been hostile to the use of third-party software that would allow Cricut owners to cut out patterns and operate the machine independently of Provo Craft's proprietary cartridges. Cricut's 'restricted to cutting designs from a collection of cartridges' was cited as a major drawback in an analysis of biting, another brand of dust-cutting machines; however, the analysis also noted that this limitation might be a preference for certain users. Construct the Cut (MTC) and Craft Edge's Certain Cuts A Lot (SCAL) were two projects that could once be used to make and then get Cricut machines to erase subjective designs. In April 2010, Provo Craft initiated legal action against the makers of "Make the Cut," and in January 2011, it sued "Craft Edge" to prevent the distribution of the SCAL software. Both times, the wholesalers reached an agreement with Provo Craft and discontinued their Cricut support. The plans may still be used with various home cutters.

'Provo Craft utilizes multiple approaches to encode as well as a cloud the USB correspondences between 'Cricut Design Studio' [a design program included with the hardware] and the Cricut e-shaper, to secure Provo Craft's restrictive scripting and firmware, as well as to avoid endeavors to capture the cutting commands,' the company claims in its legal complaint in contradiction of Craft Edge.

Provo Craft said that Craft Edge had broken the terms of its 'End User License Agreement by disassembling the Design Studio software in order to understand and mimic this shadowy custom, therefore violating copyright law. Additionally, Provo Craft confirmed that Craft Edge had harmed its Cricut trademark by claiming that its product was compatible with machines made by Provo Craft. Provo Craft stated that this would "cause confusion, misstep, or double interacting with regards to the source, or genesis of the defendant's commodities or benefits and was likely to erroneously advise a patronage, association, permit, or relationship of the plaintiff's products and businesses with Provo Craft."

Since there was no longer any software support for older versions of Cricut machines, customers were left high and dry after their devices reached "power sunset."

1.4 Cricut Cutting Machine Models

The manufacturing of Cricut machines is the responsibility of the corporation known as Provo Craft & Novelty, Inc. Utah is the location of Provo Craft's corporate headquarters. Since it was founded on December 21st, 2003, this business has remained in operation for the whole of its 17-year existence. You may choose from a wide variety of various options when it comes to purchasing electrical goods.

Tools used in machining for cutting. Every one of them has the same characteristics, and each year sees the launch of brand-spanking-new variations of them.

The electronic devices listed below are some of our favorites; nevertheless, in order to determine which one is best for you, it is imperative that you respond to the following poll as soon as possible:

Cricut Joy

 The Cricut Joy is an updated model that, in comparison to its predecessor, is both smaller (it measures 5 inches by 8 inches) and lighter (it weighs less than 4 pounds). The Cricut Joy stands apart from the rest of Cricut's product selection because it has two additional characteristics that are not offered by any other Cricut machine. The Joy is capable of cutting individual templates that are up to four feet long, and it can produce repeated cuts that are up to twenty feet long when certain devices and materials are used. The youngest member of the Cricut cutting machines community is Cricut Joy. It is the tiniest intelligent cutting machine by Cricut (gauging just 8.5 inches wide, 5 inches deep, and 5 inches high), making it extremely compact, easy to transport, and beautifully portable. While this little fellow has some real state-of-the-art capability that will encourage you to build like no other machine in the Cricut family, never let her tiny size deceive you. Cricut Joy also slices and writes, like most Cricut devices, but uses an entire host of instruments and components specially built for its limited footprint. All for Cricut Joy is well little but most significantly, purposely built to minimize fuss and irritation, thus optimizing convenience and seamless performance, ranging from vinyl's & papers to iron-on and card kits.

Anything for Cricut Joy, to be transparent here, is specially curated pens, blades, pads, fabrics, charging cable. While other items that you might have on hand can be cut down to match Cricut Joy's mats, with Cricut Joy, any Maker/Explore knives, mats, instruments, pens, etc., cannot be used. Often search for "Cricut Joy" specifically marked on the package to ensure what you're using with compatible. Until now, it was sufficient to stick some kind of material (paper, vinyl, iron-on, etc.) to an adhesive mat and afterward load the mat into the machine to cut on a Cricut machine. If the slicing design were completed, you would unload the pad, extract the material from the mat, and clean it (very often). Cricut Joy, indeed, replaces the whole operation. Underneath the feed manuals, it includes 9+ triggers that permit Cricut Joy Smart Materials to be cut without even a mat. Close to how you will install a molding machine, you literally feed these particular materials straight into the machine, and the template would be cut with the same accuracy as any other Cricut machine.

Cricut Maker

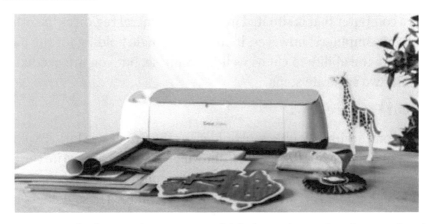

For use with the Design Room, which is a piece of software that is hosted in the cloud, the Cricut Maker desktop computer is necessary. It is not capable of functioning on its own. You will not be able to use Design Space on a personal computer (whether it be a desktop or a laptop) unless you are connected to the internet. If you use the offline features of that software by using the Design Space app on an iOS smartphone, you will be able to use your computer and layout space even if you do not have an online connection. This is because you will not need to connect to the internet in order to do so (iPad or iPhone). The Cricut Builder is a multipurpose machine that comes pre-assembled with a selection of cutting and scoring heads of varying sizes.

Cricut Explore Air 2

Its slicing speed has been increased thanks to a minor improvement that was performed in the air, and it is now twice as quick. It comes in a number of colors, and the most recent version of the Circuit Design Space application is compatible with it. You can get it here. A gadget known as the Cricut Explore Air is capable, amongst other things, of transforming paper and several other materials into the fabric. It does not need wires. It is compatible with the application that was developed specifically for the Circuit Design Space environment.

Cricut Explore Air

It is a computer that is situated in the same general region as the other Explore computers; however, it only has a single holding for the tool. You have the ability to cut as well as compose, but you are needed to do it in two separate steps.

Cricut Explore Air 1

Each comes with a double tool holder for the Cricut Explore, Explore Air, and Explore Air 2 machines, allowing you to cut and write (or cut and score) in a single action. This holder is compatible with the Cricut Explore, Explore Air, and Explore Air 2 machines. These holders are suitable for use with the Cricut Explore, Cricut Explore Air, and Cricut Explore Air 2 machines. You just need one tool holder for the Explore One, which gives you the ability to cut and write (or cut and score) on two distinct levels. Because Bluetooth was developed for the Explore Air and Explore Air 2, you will need a Cricut Wireless Bluetooth Transmitter for the Explore One and Explore if you want to use it with an Android or iOS smartphone or if you want to wirelessly disconnect it from your phone. Additionally, if you want to use it with a computer, you will need a Cricut Wireless Bluetooth Receiver for the Explore One and Explore.

Chapter 02: Methods For Using Cricut Design Space

Signing up for an account will allow you to access your previously stored designs, projects, payment details, and linked cartridges. The process is simple and straightforward; allow me to share the details with you.

Building a Cricut ID is the first order of business. First, fill out the required fields with your name and email address. Then, choose your country of origin from the dropdown menu and go to the next step.

Choose the United States or the closest option to your real location if you are not in any of these three nations. Please take a moment to read over and become familiar with the Cricut terms of service before checking the box indicating your acceptance of them. To get Cricut tutorials, inspiration, and deals through email, check the box located at the bottom of the page before giving the information.

About once per week, Cricut will drop a mail with discounts, product announcements, inspirational quotes, and other content. You may choose at any moment not to receive these types of messages by simply deselecting the corresponding box.

You should keep the box selected if you wish to proceed with the test. You may unsubscribe at any time by clicking the link in the email's bottom, or you can modify your preferences in your account. After you have completed the necessary steps, choose "Create User ID."

After you confirm your new high score, you may go on. On the next page, Cricut will give you a few questions to narrow down the search.

These are optional questions designed to give Cricut a better idea of who uses their products. Click the most applicable option from the list below. Download the Cricut Design Space add-on now.

That is the application software that will serve as the basis for your Cricut planning. To download, just click the button.

The installation process is automatically accompanied by a setup wizard.

- Choose the "Next" option.

- To show your agreement with the use terms, choose the "I accept the understanding" radio option after reading them. Before starting the download, it is needed to agree to the terms of service. Nonetheless, It is strongly advised to read the conditions before clicking the button indicating the agreement. Select "Install" to proceed.

- After that, Design Space will begin downloading and installing the following:

- After the module has finished installing, a confirmation box will appear. Once It is finished, choose "Done."

- In order to proceed, please confirm your selection on the final confirmation page.

- That's all. It is ready to power up the machine. This step is optional if you are only setting up your record without a machine. It can be activated on any machine by pressing the force catch.

After successfully connecting, choose "Continue" from the bottom right menu. Once it is connected to the Cricut to the computer, the company will check to see whether the device's software needs to be updated. Proceed by clicking the button.

Follow the on-screen prompts to begin your free two-week trial of Cricut Access and collect your prizes. You may wait to put it into effect until you have more information and then do so whenever people choose.

Having created a Cricut ID, installed the program, and updated the firmware, you are ready to either begin notating the sample job or investigate more into the capabilities of the software. Always remember to deselect the 'Remember Me option if you are using a public or shared computer. If it is chosen the "Remember Me" option, the Email/Cricut ID field won't ask for the email again.

If using a shared computer and don't want the email address compromised, people should deselect this option. On a personal computer, this field might save the trouble of typing in the email address every time somebody logs in.

To log out of the account, visit the main menu as well as click "Sign Out" at the very bottom.

Now that it is clear what "Design Space" is and how to utilize it, people can make stunning homemade items. Let's take a look at creating a "Cricut ID" so you may access "Design Space."

- Go to the 'Design' tab on the official 'Cricut' website.

- Select "Create a Cricut ID" from the drop-down menu in the new window that appears.

- At this point, it is prompted to input the individual details, such as name, surname, email address, and password, into the provided box.

- Click "Create a Cricut ID" after checking the box that reads "I agree with the Cricut Terms of Use."

- A 'New!' message and a link to the 'Design Space' homepage will immediately load for you. A machine mode selection screen will appear.

- Following the aforementioned procedures, your email address will now serve as "Cricut ID."

- Continue reading to learn how to finish signing up for "Design Space" and access its features.

- If this is the first time using "Design Space," a welcome message will appear on your screen.

- When pressing the Next button, a black screen will appear with the word "Machine" written in the upper right corner.

- If people choose "Machine," a list of Cricut machines and their available functions will appear.

2.1 Getting Started

Using the scroll bar on the right, you may explore the infinite layout options available to you inside the design area. The potential outcomes are limitless.

You don't have to be very imaginative to make stunning patterns. There are a plethora of pre-made designs available in Design Space. At the top right of the screen, where it says "Design," click here (highlighted in red). When you click here, you'll be sent to a page where you may register a new account. Simply log in with your current credentials if you have an existing account. Simply enter your details and click the "Sign In" button. By clicking this, you will be brought to the aforementioned display. This interface allows you to carry out a variety of tasks. The preceding snapshot emphasizes the most important features by highlighting them in red (menu/home, my projects, and new project). There are two options, "My Project" and "New Project," located in the upper right corner of the window. Simply click the "My Projects" link to see all of your previously saved work.

You may create them from scratch or modify existing ones in this way. However, if you want to begin a new project, you may do so by selecting the "New Project" option. As you continue reading, we'll go into greater detail about this. In addition to the tabs, the scroll bar provides quick access to the available highlighted projects.

Keep scrolling up to view other highlighted patterns. Get lost in the site and let your eyes feast on the fantastic creations, any of which may be altered to suit your needs. The menu button appears in the upper left corner of the display.

When you click it, you'll get a drop-down menu with options like "Home," "Canvas," and so on. Select the canvas by clicking the three dashes in the upper left corner of the screen next to the menu; here is where your designs will be worked on before being sent to your Cricut. Then, in the menu that appears, choose Canvas.

2.2 Surface Area of the Canvas

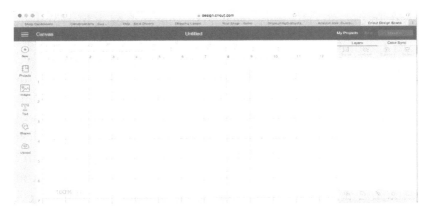

The canvas in "Design Space" should be seen as a blank slate onto which to test and realize your ideas. People have the freedom to make as many revisions to their projects as they want, adding new content such as photos and text until they're satisfied. The canvas is where you will be investing the most time with this program. At \ first sight, it seems frightening and overwhelming, although with time \ you will have a clear knowledge of the various symbols, buttons, and choices on \ this screen. Plus, you always have this book to help you. As can be seen, I've divided the screen into four portions for easier reading and comprehension.

Left Panel

This includes the main insert area with all the functions, such as the New

- Templates
- Projects
- Images
- Text
- Shape
- Upload

Top Menu Panel

This is the location most of the tools you need to edit your project are placed. In the next chapters, we'll go further into each instrument.

Right Layer Panel

Includes the layer panel. A design contains as many layers as there are objects, shapes, images, and texts in it. Each new design element you add will have its own layer in the layer panel. The section of the canvas in the center indicated by the number 4 is where your design will appear as you work on it. The area shown by the gridlines in the preceding picture represents this region. This will walk you through the four primary portions of this painting. We'll go through every conceivable graphic, control, and setting. Maintain your course of study. First, we'll look at the left side of the page.

New

This is the primary menu selection to the left. Choose this path if you want to launch a brand-new endeavor. If you click on it, a fresh blank page will open up. Whether you are already in the middle of a project and you click the "New" button, a window will appear asking if you want to preserve your work or start again with a blank canvas.

Template

The template will appear as the second option on your canvas's left sidebar. When you choose this icon, you'll be sent to a page where you can choose from a wide variety of premade layouts to get a good idea of how your design will look on a variety of different surfaces. Choose a premade design for inspiration, then modify it to suit your needs. Let's pretend you're interested in adding a personalized message on your shirt. It's as easy as picking a shirt design, tweaking the proportions to your liking, and entering some text. Once you've decided where on the shirt you want the text to go, you can go on to Step 2.

Note: The templates themselves cannot be printed out or stored. However, they are helpful since they allow you to picture your design and serve as a reference when putting up the size, height, space, and other qualities. To start a project, a template is unnecessary. However, if you want to see your design in 3D on a surface, a template is the way to go. It's possible to alter the size of a template while editing it. This is in the upper left section of the template you've chosen. When you click on a template, the canvas will automatically load it so that you may start working with it right away. At this point, you may modify the chosen template's 'Type,' 'Size,' and 'Color' by clicking the corresponding buttons that appear directly above the canvas area. Get the template just as you want it with the help of these settings. Tasks This section of the design studio is my favorite. Under the 'Projects' tab, you'll find a wide variety of pre-made layouts to choose from. You don't have to be a creative pro to come up with a great design with this feature. Simply choose the 'Project' tab to get started. If you click this, a window displaying all the templated projects will pop up. Just scroll down to the desired layout and click "Make It" or "Customize It" to have it created.

Take note that the "Make It" button is conveniently located in the upper right corner of the screen. It is appreciated that you can alter the settings for any of the available projects or just press "Make It" to generate a layout. That's cool, right?

It's important to remember that not all of the offerings are gratis. Even though most of the projects require the purchase of Cricut supplies, users of Cricut Access get access to the majority of the designs. Your Cricut access membership gives you access to all projects marked with a little green a. Those who don't want to pay for a Cricut access membership may still buy individual projects. Once you've paid for a design, you may use it whenever you want, as often as you like. But with Cricut, there's no need to spend money on a premade pattern at all. As a newbie, you may choose from a wide variety of free templates. If it is just starting off, it is suggested to pick one of the many free projects to experiment with. Use the menu to the right of the search bar at the top of the Project screen to narrow your result. By choosing a subcategory of projects from this menu, you may refine your search results. In the upper right corner of your screen, you'll see a drop-down menu labeled "All Categories." Click it, and have a look at what you may find. There will never be enough of them.

Images

Going down the left side is the 'Images' option. You may add pictures to your design with the help of the image tool. Consider the following scenario: I'd want to create a teddy bear-themed tablecloth. After selecting the "Image" tab, I'll go through the presented photos until I locate one of the teddy bears that I can use in my design.

Alternatively, you may conduct a more precise search by using the specialized options provided by the search button's drop-down menu (found in the upper right corner of the screen). Simply enter your search terms (teddy bear, for example) into the box and hit the "search" button.

The 'Cartridges' and 'Categories' buttons in the upper right-hand corner of the screen may also be used to narrow down your picture search. If you hold a Cricut Access membership and see a green 'a symbol on an image, you may use it. You'd have to pay to use any more pictures you wanted. The fact that fresh photographs are uploaded to the gallery every week is another fantastic feature of the 'Images' tab. As a result, you may keep making unique designs without worrying about running out of suitable photos. One step farther down the list is the 'Text' option. There are a lot of uses for this crucial instrument. Mastering this tool in its entirety may take some time, but with repeated use, you will quickly find that it becomes less of a challenge.

When you choose the "Text" tool, a blank page with a text box will appear. The text you enter in the box will appear on the canvas. In the following image, It is altered the color of the text from its normal black to purple.

The second thing you'll see is a sophisticated menu bar labeled "Edit Menu" emerge in the top panel of the screen when you pick the text tool and begin typing. People will find all the tools and shortcuts you'll need to format and modify your text in the menu bar at the top of the screen. Please allow me to walk you through the top panel now.

In the upper left of the textual edit window, people will see a pull-down menu labeled "Font." If people click on it, then they will be able to choose a new typeface for the text. Cricut fonts and system fonts are only two examples of the multitudes of font types available.

People may also use the list of available fonts to choose one that works for the design by simply scrolling down the page. In the upper right corner of the same text menu panel, they'll find a search field where they may key in the name of the font family they're interested in, the name of the exact font they're looking for, or both. By narrowing the results in this way, you may quickly choose typefaces that meet your needs. If we write 'System Fonts,' for instance, into the search field, I'll only get results for the fonts that are currently installed on my computer.

Everybody should now be able to pick typefaces and switch between font styles with ease. Let's get through this! Most of the tools needed to alter the text in creative potential may be found in the top tool menu. In this section, you'll discover the tools you need to change the properties of your text and customize its appearance in your layout. People may change things like font size, font style, line spacing, letter spacing, orientations, and so on.

The down and up arrows are the primary controls for this set of tools. So, to make text smaller, for example, use the down arrow. However, if they'd want to make the typeface larger, people may do so by pressing the up arrow until they're happy with the outcome. Most text editors follow this guideline. In the next chapters,

It is shown in detail how to use every option available in the main editing menu. Hold tight for more developments. The 'Isolate Layer' option is another helpful tool. One may use this to split a single letter from a string of text so that it can be revised independently. One letter may have its size increased. The font changed, the letter rotated, etc. Select the text on the canvas, right-click the mouse, and choose 'Ungroup' from the menu that appears to separate the letters.

One may now take your time with each letter and make it exactly as you want it. When done and happy with the results, people may need to regroup the letters so that you may continue to modify the text as a whole (by moving, editing, rotating, etc.). Pick the text people want to group, then select 'Group' from the menu that appears.

We've been exploring the canvas's left panel tools so far. The shape tool follows the text tool on the toolbar. Do people understand all that has been said thus far? Relax for a while. One should pick up just where people left off when one returns.

By the time you finish reading, you'll understand everything.

Shape

The form tool allows you to, well, insert shapes into your layout. You may choose from roughly 9 different forms, like squares, circles, hearts, stars, triangles, and so on. The capacity to put your own spin on things is what makes working with shapes so interesting. You may personalize them in a variety of ways, from changing their color to resizing and rotating them. The options are unlimited, as you will discover later on in this book.

The above basic layout was created by combining the 'Shape' feature, the 'Text' tool, and the 'Images' feature. What I did is as follows:

- Select the "Text" menu item and enter "HELLO WORLD."

- Then, move the text to where you want it to appear using the arrow keys.

- Third, click and drag the 'Resize' handle in the bottom right corner of the text box to make the text larger or smaller.

- Select "Text Color" from the main menu to make a change.

- Find the 'Curve' tool in the top edit menu panel, and move the curve slider to the right. As can be seen above, doing this operation causes my text to curl upwards.

- Select the square form by clicking the "Shape" tab.

- Select a shape, then use the resizing lever in its lower right corner to make adjustments to its size.

- Follow step eight: right-click the form, then choose "Send to Back." The chosen shape will be moved to the end of the current text.

- Use the top edit menu panel to alter the shape's color.

- Ten. Select "Images" from the menu on the left.

- Eleven. Find a picture that appeals to you and click it.

- Then, drag the image's handle to make it smaller, then drop it into the square.

- Clicking the relevant layer in the layer panel will allow you to make changes to each color in the chosen shape (right panel).

The next section goes into further detail on this topic. The examples shown above are just the tip of the iceberg of what you may do with your newfound knowledge. Continue reading, and we'll go into further detail about the 'Curve' tool, the 'Send to Back feature, and more.

Upload

This is the last canvas tool on the left side. When you choose it, you'll be sent to a page where you may select designs or pictures already on your computer to be cut using your Cricut. Additionally, you may find a wide variety of ready-made patterns online, which you can then import into design space, modify as desired, and cut. Let's suppose, therefore, that there is already some kind of form or pattern on your canvas. When you have this element chosen, you'll see that in each of its four corners, you'll find a unique icon. The first icon is a little 'x' in the upper left corner. At any point, you may utilize this to completely seal the form or piece.

A padlock symbol appears in the design's lower left corner. It's utilized when resizing an element to keep its original aspect ratio. Any time you decide you no longer wish to keep the ratios the same, just click the padlock. The rotation handle is located in the upper right corner of the form or design element. The slider to adjust the size of the form is located in the upper left corner.

A few terms will need to be clarified before we can get into the step-by-step approach to using the 'Edit Bar' in the Design Space. Some of the phrases used here are typical tools for daily usage on the computer, so it shouldn't be too challenging to grasp; nonetheless, our degree of computer knowledge may not be the same. Consequently, I apologize in advance if you currently know most of them. Those who are unaware of this have prompted us to take this action. The following are the conditions:

Undo/Redo

This means reverting back to a prior version of the layer or reversing an action that was previously undone.

Line type

It describes how the device will cut, draw, and score the paper on the mat. When you cut anything, you remove a section of it from your material by slicing it with a blade.

Sketch

This means you used a Cricut pen to draw the layer. Marking the layer that used a scoring stylus or marking wheel. A swatch of the line kind.

Selecting supplementary properties for your layer. Your choices will vary depending on whatever option(s) you choose.

Line type

Cricut Design Space's creators have included signs when a certain choice is selected to help you immediately recognize what you've chosen. If you choose to cut, Score, or Draw, for instance, the swatch will take on a solid, /, or outline appearance.

Reducing Characteristics

When the 'Cut' line type is chosen, these options will become accessible.

Advance

You may use it to choose a color from the color picker that you've created. The hexadecimal value for the chosen color may also be input.

Incorporate Characteristics

When the "Draw" line type is used, these options will be shown. From the menu that appears, choose the Cricut pen. The list will adapt to show the available colors for the chosen pen type.

Fill

These are the colors or patterns that will be employed to fill the picture layers before they are sent to the printer.

Vacant Space

This is how you remove the layer from a picture without destroying it. As a result, it may be used to switch from the Fill mode to the Cut mode once the Fill mode has been applied to the layer.

Print

When selecting 'Print and Cut,' here is where you'll look for the available color and pattern selections.

Fill Swatch

Used for customizing the picture layer with 'Fill' properties like color and pattern for 'Print Then Cut' images.

Artwork That Is Truly Unique

By selecting this option, all changes you made to a "Print" layer will be undone. Color Choose the 'Print then Cut' color from the standard color palette, a custom color picker, the currently available material colors, or by entering the hex color code in this field.

Fill patterns may be applied to a text layer or an image with this. Color filters may be used for the 'Narrow Patterns' search, and the 'Edit Pattern' tools can be used to modify the pattern's size and position in the picture.

This toggles between selecting and deselecting anything on the canvas at once. You may utilize Edit This to look for common editing functions like cut, copy, and paste. You can cut an image to save it for later, copy it, and then paste it into the canvas using the corresponding buttons; cut, copy, and paste are all located in the editing toolbar at the top.

Align

It's used to set the relative placement of two or more pictures or objects inside a specified margin. The pictures may be arranged in a number of different ways, including left, right, top, and bottom (horizontally or vertically). What follows is a breakdown of the settings available in this app's menu bar.

Set to the Left

This feature allows you to align several pictures or objects to the left edge. The object's left edge on the canvas will be affected. An item's horizontal center is defined by this, and its effects are perceived in the precise horizontal center of a set of items (the central point).

Placement on the Right

Here, you may set the vertical distance between two or more items in the right margin. When this option is used, its effects will be felt on the rightmost edge of the rightmost item in the selection. This setting allows you to align the top margin with your photos or other items. The tip-top edge of the most recently chosen objects/images will feel its impact.

Vertical Center

By selecting this option, you may align many photos or objects with the center of the vertical space. When you pick this option, the impact will be concentrated in the precise vertical center of the chosen items or photos.

Justify the Footing

When two or more photos or other objects are chosen, the bottom margin may be used to adjust their relative position, with the adjustment taking effect at the object's bottommost edge.

Center

By selecting this option, you may align the chosen items' centers with one another. It's also used when superimposing several photos.

Horizontal dispersal

Selecting this option allows you to arrange the photos such that they flank the object's left and right sides in an equal manner.

Spread Horizontally

Using this option, you may disperse the chosen objects such that they are equidistant from the top and bottom boundaries of the canvas.

Reverse Send

In the same way, as the name suggests, pressing this button moves the currently chosen item to the bottom of the stack. In this case, the item will sink to the bottom of the 'Layers Panel.'

Go in reverse

By selecting this menu item, the item you've chosen will be pushed to the bottom of the stack.

Continue onward

Use this to advance the layer the chosen item is on in the stack. As a result, the layer the item is on will advance by one.

Forward Orders

By clicking here, the item you've chosen will be brought to the top of the stack. By doing so, the item will now be shown in the 'Layers Panel's primary position.

Flip

You may adjust the object's orientation by using this button. Because of this, it has the "Flip Horizontal" and "Flip Vertical" options.

Size

The height and width of the chosen item may be adjusted here by entering new values or by using the stepper tool to make adjustments in 0.1 increments.

Keep in mind that while the object's size is fixed, adjusting its width and height will also affect its depth and other properties in proportion.

Unlocking the image's aspect ratio allows you to make separate adjustments to the object's width and height.

Use the stepper to make little, 1-degree adjustments, or enter the precise angle you want to give the item using the Rotate option.

More

In case your screen is too small to display all of the editing tools, this will display them for you. When you click this, the edit bar's hidden tools will appear in a drop-down menu.

Position

Choose this to move the chosen item by either typing in the new coordinates relative to the top left corner of the canvas or using the steppers to zoom in or out by 0.1-pixel increments. The Windows/Macintosh Procedure for Creating a Line type.

Type in Your Content or Drop Your Images Into The Template. The 'Line type' menu may be accessed from the 'Edit' menu. Take note of how the kind of line that is active is highlighted. Multiple layers' line types may be altered at once by selecting them and then choosing a new line type first from the drop-down menu.

Once you make your pick, the canvas's picture will update to reflect it. To utilize "Print then Cut," choose "Fill" from the menu's drop-down menu. In that window, click "Print." Choose a color or pattern from the 'Fill' swatch menu to fill the layer with that hue or design.

If your project has many levels and the line type is configured to "Write" or "Score," the picture must be placed on a different layer. To achieve this, choose the two levels you want to attach in the 'Layers' panel and then click the 'Attach' button.

2.3 Modifying Fonts in Adobe Design Space

One of Cricut Design Space's many perks is the option to add custom text and fonts to your creations. Explain what makes this special for the simple reason that it allows your imagination to go wild. Humans are born with a natural capacity for creativity, and when the efforts are completed to our satisfaction, we experience a profound feeling of pride and fulfillment. After ungrouping or isolating the letters, you may change the font in Cricut Design Space; you can use the Cricut fonts or the fonts already on your computer or device.

2.4 Cricut Design Space

The space is, in essence, and in more ways than one, analogous to a portable printer used with a laptop. You send the pattern to the computer much as you would to a printer, but instead of depositing ink on a piece of paper, the computer spins a blade around enough to cut through the information you have sent it have made their choice.

Adding Text

To add text, go to the canvas's left side and click the 'Text' tool. The 'Text' option is found in the bottom left corner of the app screen on iOS and Android devices. Selecting the text tool on iOS/Android will bring up a selection of available fonts; on Windows/Mac, the text bar and text box will appear. First, choose the font and size you want to use, and then enter your text. Use the Return key at the end of a line of text in the same textbox to begin a new line of text. On a Windows or Mac computer, you may input the text before picking the font in Cricut Design Space, so there's no need to panic if you forget to choose the font first. How long has it been since we last spoke about this? Yes, of course you do. To dismiss the input box, just click or press anywhere else on the screen.

Change Text in Cricut Design Space

Adding text to the canvas is the first step you've completed. Make any necessary changes to the text at this point. The text may be resized, shifted, and rotated in a variety of ways. Use this straightforward method to modify the canvas's existing text.

It's easy to make changes to the text. To see the possible choices, just double-click the text. Select the desired action from the available choices, which may include font style. Modify the line spacing, letter spacing, and font size. The Edit menu is where you'll find all of these controls.

If you're using a PC or Mac, you'll see the Edit bar at the very top of the canvas; on iOS and Android, it'll be at the very bottom.

2.5 A Guide to Choosing a Font

The 'Text Edit Tool' in Cricut Design Space is quite similar to the 'Image Edit Tool,' so users who are familiar with that feature will feel right at home with it. This is due to the fact that both programs have a similar method of operation for adjusting the rotation, size, and location of text. You'll be thrilled by the similarities between the tools, as this will make your work editing text and choosing a font much easier. You may add your own flair to tasks using this.

Do you know what a bounding box is? If you haven't heard, I'll fill you in.

Selecting some text causes a box to appear around it; this is called the bounding box. It resembles the text box border more closely, except in this instance, there are rounded "handles" at each of the four corners of the bounding box. The text may be quickly repositioned, resized, deleted, and its aspect ratio locked or unlocked with these controls.

As previously mentioned, the Edit tab in Cricut Design Space enables you to change specific aspects of selected pictures and text. You can change things like the line's thickness, color, location, rotation, and reflection. You may change the line spacing, font, and letter spacing in the 'Text layers' section. Is there a way to change the font?

This is where I'll demonstrate it to you. Choose the text item on the canvas that you want to modify, add text using the design panel's "Insert Text" option, or open a text layer using the "Layers Panel." When you choose it, a new bar labeled "Text Edit Bar" will appear underneath the "Standard Edit Bar."When you are not editing the text, the "Standard Edit Bar" will disappear.

When the "Text Edit Bar" appears, you may start changing the font using the tools shown below. Easy, right?

Font

It's possible to see the computer's default fonts in addition to the Cricut fonts using this option. Soon, we'll talk about the system typefaces that are available.

Use a Condensed Font Size

Depending on the parameters you choose, this will display a menu of possible choices. You may choose to see simply the Cricut fonts or the System fonts \sinstalled on the computer, or even view all the fonts combined. Here, you can \salso select to search for fonts or apply a filter to the fonts by scrolling \ through the font list to find the one that suits your requirements.

2.6 Filter Typeface

You may choose your preferred fonts according to their classification in the 'Font Type' drop-down box. The following is a list and explanation of some of the font filters available:

TrueType, OpenType, and Other Fonts: This shows all the available typefaces for you.

Fonts on the System

This will show the fonts that are installed on your machine. Here you may see the fonts that are available in the Cricut font collection. The typefaces shown below are single-layer types, meaning that there is only one layer to them.

Style

Font styles such as italic, bold, normal, bold italic, and writing style may be selected with this menu item. Keep in mind that the typeface you're using will affect the available formatting choices (Cricut font or System Font)

Typeface Magnitude

The point size of the typeface may be changed using this option. Point size may be set by either typing in a numeric number or by using the steppers to make small, incremental adjustments.

Letter Spacing Here, you may adjust the distance between individual characters.

Similarly, to the font size, you can either manually enter a value or utilize the steppers to make incremental changes.

Negative Spatial Context Linear

Here, you may adjust the distance between successive columns of text. As before, you may either manually enter the value or utilize the steppers to get there.

Alignment

All of the text in the block may be aligned to the left, right, center or fully justified using this feature.

Curve

By doing so, you may make the text form a circle. A maker of rounded objects like cups, bowls, and pails might benefit from this choice.

Advanced

Separate blocks of text, characters, lines, and even whole text layers may now be created in this way. Two sub-options are available inside this choice, as shown below:

The Ungroup to Letters option allows you to turn the letters in the text box into individual images that can be found in the Layers Panel. The individual letter layers may be edited separately while the overall structure is preserved.

Text in a text box may be ungrouped into individual lines by selecting the Ungroup to Lines option, which then appears as individual layers in the Layers Panel. Similar to the Ungroup to Letters, you may make individual changes to the lines while still maintaining their original grouping.

2.7 Formatting Your Writing Using Typefaces

In Cricut Design Space, you may use a pen and special typefaces to create a wide variety of lettering. Changing the line type of your text from 'Cut' to 'Write' in Cricut Design Space allows you to easily write any font using Cricut pens with any Cricut machine that is compatible with Cricut Design Space (Cricut Maker and Cricut Explore series). The next step is to pick the 'Writing style' you like and the font you want to use. Keep in mind that the Cricut machine will trace the edges of the letters rather than writing them directly due to the typefaces used in the writing style. You have gained an understanding of how to write with typefaces and how those fonts will ultimately look. I can see that Cricut Design Space is quickly becoming one of your favorite tools. Please hold on, and there's more information to come.

2.8 Color Matching Software

If you're familiar with Design Space, you'll know that the 'Color Sync' tool, like the 'Flatten' tool, has more than one purpose. Some of the things that it can do are listed below.

- Recoloring forms, layers, etc., is possible using the Color Sync tool.

- It may be used to harmonize the hues of every canvas layer.

- Coordinating hues across several materials, it's invaluable.

- Use of this tool results in significant material and labor savings.

The earlier Design Space versions lacked this capability. Nonetheless, since it is already in the updated version, why not use it for some exploits?

With this app, it's much simpler to coordinate a project's color palette so that different shapes may be cut from the same sheet of paper. Simply click on the "Color Sync" panel on the right side of the screen, and then drag and drop each form onto the layer you want it to synchronize with. Select all the stars you want to remove from the chartreuse layer and then use the 'Color Sync' panel to move the remaining stars to the same layer. Having them all be the same hue makes this process so much more reassuring.

2.9 Creating a Rough Draft in the Design Area

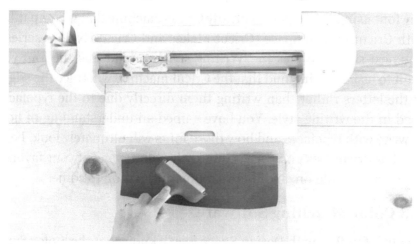

Amazingly, users of the Cricut Explore model may upload not only pre-made graphics but also ones they have generated themselves! To do this, you may utilize either Illustrator or Design Space. And because we're talking about the Design Space, I'll focus on the latter and explain how to achieve it. Specifically, these steps are taken:

Importing the desired picture into your computer is the first step. If you'd rather sketch what you need by hand instead of using a tablet, you may do so and then either scan the drawing into your computer, take a picture of it with your mobile device and upload it, or save it and upload it through your tablet. Save the file as a PNG or JPEG, no matter what method you choose. Next, submit the picture to Design Space by clicking the "Upload" link on the left side of the screen. There will be a prompt asking you to choose an image type; pick the one that best describes your picture's context. After your picture has been properly cropped, you may proceed by choosing "Continue" and saving it as a "Cut" image. Your picture is now saved as a 'Cut' file, which you can easily recognize.

And that's how you get your drawing into Design Space and start editing it! You can really go crazy with your imagination while using this feature. So much can be accomplished by using just your hands! Since the Design Space environment places no constraints on your creativity, don't ever feel that you have to.

Chapter 03: Project Planning

By utilizing the Flattening tool in the design space, you may convert any picture into a printable one for use with the Print then Cut function. It's helpful to flatten the picture into a single layer.

3.1 Flattening Tool

However, if the image is multilayered, the "Unflatten" tool may be used to recover the original layers that were flattened during the enhancement process. No layer printing is possible inside the app. To counter this, the program allows for the layered design of print projects. So, you'll need to make use of design space on your computer to do the task.

Altering the line type of a layer may transform it into a printed picture. The word "Print" will be printed in a different font. To learn more about the various line types available, check out the Layer> Changing Line type option. The flatten function allows you to combine many photos into one printable file.

3.2 Converting Images and Layers to a Flatter Format

Useful for altering regular photos into printed ones. Both the regular and the improved printable pictures may be manipulated to seem better by printing them side by side.

- Select a standard image (of any kind) from the Cricut image library, open the image panel by selecting the image button, and insert the picture into your current project. When using Design Space, a flattened picture may be uploaded and used.

- As a second step, you should utilize the 'Layer' button to bring up the layer panel. Press the "Action" button to bring up the contextual menu.

- Third, pick the layers (two or more) you want to merge into one.

- In the fourth step, you'll click the "Flatten" button in the action panel to prepare the layers for printing. When a layer is flattened, all of its sublayers collapse into a single layer on the layer panel, and the name will change to read "Flattened Sets." You may also print and cut, as shown by the printer icon next to the layer thumbnail.

The image's line layer has to be in the 'Cut' mode before you can use the flatten tool. In the layer panel, you may alter the line type by clicking the corresponding button.

3.3 Creating Disparaging Versions of Stock Photos

When editing an unpleasant picture in Cricut design space, you may divide a conventional image into distinct layers.

To begin, choose the 'Layer' and 'Action' buttons to see the Layer and Action panels, respectively. The next thing to do is choose the picture you want to flatten. Unflatten the merged picture by clicking the corresponding button in the layers panel. How to Make Enhanced Multilayered Printable Images Unattractive.

By unflattening the file in the Design Space, multilayered, improved printable graphics may be separated into individual layers. First, choose the "Image" option to bring up the image input window. Open the filter menu and choose "Multilayer." Pick out some high-quality, printable cricket pictures from the collection. You can tell that a picture has been upgraded for printing by looking for the printer symbol in the tile's upper left corner. The second stage entails picking out the picture. Select the 'Floating' button in the action panel to divide the flattened picture into individual layers, as seen in the Layer panel. Some layers in the layers panel may have an icon depicting an eye with a line across it; this indicates that the Layer is hidden. Using the 'Hiding' and 'Unhiding' buttons in the layers panel will provide further information.

3.4 Using Text in Work

It's simple and straightforward to give your project a unique look and feel by adding text and various faces in the Circuit design environment. To modify the wording to your liking, please visit the following pages. First, on the device's design screen, pick the text tab, which is to the left of the canvas [in the design panel]. Doing so will bring up a blank text box with an edit field where you may type your content. Second, after you've selected the 'Text Edit' field, you may start typing your text, and when it displays in the textbox below, you can hit the return key on your keyboard to make line breaks. The name of the team may be deduced from the first few characters of the text in the layer panel. The first letter of each text layer serves as a symbol as well. In Step 3, click on the dark area of any letter to simply move it on the canvas and adjust its size and orientation as you see fit.

When you pick some text, a box will appear around it. You may use the edges of this box to make quick and easy changes. Select the text by clicking on the solid region of each letter to reveal its bounding box. The text may be removed from the design screen by clicking the red x at the top left corner of the bounding box. Once you do this, the text will no longer be visible in the design window and will be permanently removed from the layers panel. Text may be rotated by grabbing its rotation handle (top right) and dragging it to a new place inside the bounding box; any changes you make to the text's position will be reflected in the grey army Decatur that appears next to the picture.

If you look closely in the bottom left corner of the volume box, you'll see a closed lock symbol. This indicates that you may alter the width and height while maintaining a fixed ratio and that the text will be saved in the same fashion. An erroneous click on the aspect ratio will unlock it for you. This allows you to resize images in InDesign without worrying about maintaining their aspect ratio and adjusting their width and height separately. By clicking and holding the seasoned handle in the lower right corner of the bounding box, you may lock or unlock the text's proportions and then drag it in any direction to observe how the text resizes automatically.

Fourth, to alter the font size, click and drag the seasoned handle located in the lower right corner of the enclosing box.

3.5 Methods for Including Pictures in Cricut Design Space

- First, go to the design panel on the left side of the canvas to access the Cricut image collection. If you follow the instructions, a new window will open up, and all of the photographs in the collection, including the Cricut images, will be shown there. Images may be picked, flipped through, searched for, and filtered.

- Second, a variety of picture tiles will appear on display. Choose a suitable picture file to import into the canvas. A green sibling will show once you choose the picture file. This demonstrates how easily the picture may be integrated into your 'Image' tree at the display's base.

Please note that you may choose and upload several photos simultaneously.

You may get more details about the picture by clicking the I button. Access level, picture number, and anything else relevant to the image is provided. Anti All the mages' outfits are on sale, so if you like what you see, you may buy it right now.

Furthermore, you may click on the cartridge's name to get further picture details. Also, the symbol for returning to the previous page is always at your disposal.

- Third, click the "Insert Image" option after picking the desired photos to bring them into the canvas.

- To delete a picture from the image tray, hover over the image until a red 'x' appears, then click the 'x' to select the image and then click the Delete button.

- Reposition and resize the picture in your project as needed. You may wish to check out the finer points of a picture on occasion. To achieve this, click the option labeled "See Image Formation" located in the panel's header.

If you want to reuse a picture, just click its name or ID, and you'll be sent to the 'Insert Image' box.

3.6 Slicing an Image

Use this tool to disentangle overlapping photo or text layers. It's useful for making the cut path between two photos, too. All-new forms are generated in the process of four or more. A new shape layer containing all of the newly made forms will be added to the panel.

The tool also allows you to remove overlapped sections of one form from another, as well as create new shapes from previously existing ones. You may use it to remove text from any graphic. There is a limit of two layers that may be active at once when using the slice tool. When working with a multilayered picture or text, the slice tool won't be accessible until you conceal or ungroup the other levels. When using the slice feature on the design screen and layer panel, when the layers are hidden, all layers are deleted. If you want to utilize the picture of the text layer in your project, ungroup before using the slice tool.

In the first stage, the photos are organized such that they overlap. Second, while clicking on each layer, hold down the shift key to select both photos. A selection box will show up around the two photos, and the layers panel will be fully highlighted. If you choose two layers, the slice tool will immediately begin cutting between them.

Third, you'll see the newly created pictures from each split image in the layer's panel. The layers panel will no longer display hidden layers. More than three new forms may be created when two photos partly overlap; this is because the number of shapes created is proportional to the number of overlaps between the two images. Images that can be printed can be sliced using the available tools. It works equally well on pictures and graphics with patterned fills. If you want to quickly remove unwanted elements from photos, this is the tool for you.

Four split the layers to examine the modified forms. By the end of the procedure, you will have many copies of the layer-by-layer slice parts. Pictures may be changed or removed independently.

3.7 Image Contour Modification

Contouring Equipment, You may use this to conceal part of an image layer, which will also remove any relevant cut paths. To weld your repair, you must first conceal some of the text layers. When you weld your text, it merges into a single picture layer, eliminating the need for cut paths.

In order to utilize a contour, you must first ungroup the picture's layers if the image has more than one. The second step is to choose which picture layers will be used. Third, click the "Control" button in the layer panel. Your picture layer preview will load in a new window. Grayscale preview, please take note. A dark green line denotes the severed routes, while a dark grey line dominates the picture. All the represented routes are shown on the right-hand side.

In the fourth step, you may choose the unwanted picture parts by clicking on them. The picture preview will show a shift in the fill and contour of the image, and the tile will be emphasized; the tile is situated on the right side, indicating that it is no longer part of the image and will not be cut.

Please take note that you must keep at least one of the clipped pathways visible. A cut route is hidden other than its base when the option to "Hide All Contours" is selected. When you're done concealing the unwanted parts of the picture, click the "x" in the upper right corner of the screen.

Steps for Making a Canvas Reflection of an Existing Image:

There are mainly three options for you to copy a picture on the canvas

- Use keyboard shortcuts to copy and paste.

- The Edit menu's copy and paste options.

- Selecting the layer you want to duplicate and then click the 'Duplicate' button in the layer panel.

First, choose the picture you wish to copy on the canvas, which will bring up the bounding box. Once you reach the max preview page after choosing "Make It," you may duplicate the whole project as many times as you want. Next, adjust the desired number of duplicate items and hit the "Apply" button. You may use any of two methods to replicate a chosen picture. Here is a list of your potential choices:

A first choice is to simply utilize the 'Duplicate' option, which can be found in the edit menu, to create a copy of the currently chosen picture. Once you've copied the picture, you may paste it into the canvas (the currently chosen image) by clicking the "Paste" button, also found in the Edit menu. You may also make a copy of the picture by clicking the duplicate button at the very top of the layers panel (selected image). To proceed to Step 4, keep in mind that the duplicated picture will superimpose itself over the original.

Select the cloned picture before dragging it to a new location on the canvas (Step 5). Select the two copies, then duplicate them once again to make four copies of the picture on your canvas.

What to Do If You Accidentally Delete an Image in Cricut Space

Images on the canvas may be removed in three ways:

To begin with, you may utilize your computer's delete button. Click the red "x" in the bordered area.

Third, click "Delete" in the Layers panel.

First, choose the picture on the canvas that you wish to remove; this will bring up a bounding box. You may temporarily remove the picture from the design screen if you do not want to eliminate it completely. Please be aware that the mat preview will not be supplied with every concealed picture. Second, there are fast methods to get rid of the picture you choose. The first option is to use the 'delete' key on your computer keyboard to remove pictures. The second option is to erase the picture by clicking the red "x" in the top left corner of the enclosing box. Third, under the layer menu, choose the picture you want to erase and then click the 'Delete' option. Deleted images are permanently hidden from the canvas in the fourth step. Selecting several photos for deletion from the canvas at once is possible.

Chapter 04: Project Ideas

You may avoid cutting with some versions of the Cricut by using a marker instead. This enables you to write code or create drawings on your computer while using the Cricut. It works brilliantly to create invitations for events and weddings that have the appearance of being hand produced. Yet without forcing your hands into an uncomfortable position. Some people own a scoring tool that may be used for making frames, stamps, decorations, and other paper crafts of various types.

4.1 Leather Cuff Bracelet

Supplies Needed

- A small piece of leather
- A bracelet or piece of chain or cord
- small jump rings
- Needle-nose pliers for jewelry
- Deep cut blade for the Cricut Explore

Instructions

- Your first step is to choose the design image that you would like to use on your leather bracelet. This can be found inside the image files under 'Lace' or any other design file that you already have.

- Next, verify that the sizing is appropriate for a bracelet by cutting it on paper. You definitely do not want to cut the leather and be wrong. This would waste the materials.

- Once the size is perfect, you are able to begin your project.

- Place the leather on the mat with the smooth side down and push the 'Cut' button.

- After the leather piece is cut, you will need to adjust your chain or rope to the appropriate size that is needed for the wrist of the person that it will be fitting.

- Connect the leather to the chain with the jump rings. Attaching the links to the leather is perfectly fine, but it may tear the leather, so using the jump rings is a great alternative.

- This is a simple process that anyone with a Cricut and a need to make leather goods can do

4.2 Vinyl Wall Decals

Supplies Needed

- Adhesive vinyl Cricut machine
- Weeding tool Scraper tool

Instructions

- Log in to the Cricut design space.
- Create a new project.
- Click on 'Upload Image.
- Drag the image to the design space.
- Highlight the image and 'Flatten' it.
- Click on the 'Make It button.
- Place vinyl on the cutting mat.
- Custom dial the machine to vinyl.
- Load the cutting mat into the machine.
- Push the mat up against the rollers.
- Cut the design out of the vinyl.
- Weed out the excess vinyl with a weeding tool.
- Apply a thin layer of transfer tape on the vinyl.
- Peel off the backing.
- Apply the transfer tape on the wall.
- Smoothen with a scraper tool to let out the air bubbles.
- Carefully peel off the transfer tape from the wall

4.3 Wooden Hand-Lettered Sign

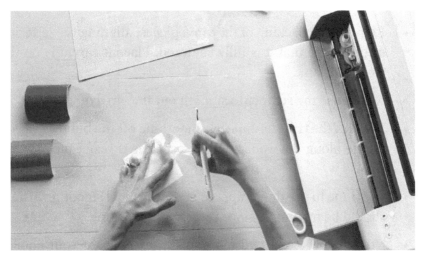

Supplies Needed

- Acrylic paint for whatever colors you would like

- Vinyl Cricut Explore Air

- Walnut hollow basswood planks

- Transfer Tape Scraper

- An SVG file or font that you wish to use Pencil Eraser

Instructions

- You will need to start by deciding what you will want to draw on the wood.

- Then, place some lines on the plank to designate the horizontal and vertical axis for the grid. Set this aside for later.

- Upload the file that you wish to use to the Design Space. Then, cut the file with the proper setting for vinyl.

- Weed out the writing or design spaces that are not meant to go on the wood.

- Using the transfer tape, apply the tape to the top of the vinyl and smooth it out. Using the scraper and the corner of the transfer paper, slowly peel the backing off a bit at a time. Do it carefully.

- Remove the backing of the vinyl pieces, aligning the lettering or design so that it is fully centered. Place it carefully on the wooden plank.

- Again, use the scraper to smooth out the vinyl on the plank.

- Take off the transfer tape by smoothing off the bubbles as you scrape along the wood sign. Discard the transfer tape at that time.

- Continue to use the scraper to make the vinyl smoother. There should be no bumps since this creates bleeding.

- Now, paint your wood plank with any color of your choice. Peel the vinyl letters off. Once the paint has completely dried, you are able to erase your pencil marks.

4.4 Cloud Coasters

Supplies Needed

- Whichever Cricut machine you have chosen to purchase
- An active account for Design Space
- A pair of scissors
- Fleece that is fusible
- An iron
- A sewing machine
- Cotton fabric
- thread to go with it

Instructions

- Grab your fabric.
- Cut your fabric and make sure it is twelve inches.

- Open your design space and hit the button that says 'New Project.'

- Click on the button that says 'Shapes' and then insert a shape that looks like a cloud. You are going to do this from the pop-up window.

- You will need to resize your cloud to five and a half inches.

- Click on the button that says 'Make It.'

- Change your project copies to four. You will have to do this so that you can have a front and back for each coaster.

- Click the button that says 'Apply.'

- Click the button that says 'Continue.'

- Adjust your settings for the materials to medium fabrics (like cotton).

- Load your mat with the attached fabric.

- Hit 'Cut.'

- Repeat three steps, but you will be placing the fleece on the cutting mat, not the fabric.

- Change your cloud shape to 5.7."

- Select a material and click where it says 'View More.'

- Then type in 'Fusible Fleece.'

- Cut out two of your fleece clouds.

- Attach one of the fleece clouds to the back of one of the fabric hearts. Use a hot iron.

- Repeat this step with the second heart.

- Place your right sides together, and then sew the clouds together. When you do this, make sure that the fleece is attached. Leave a tiny gap in the stitches for turning.

- You will now need to clip the curves.

- Turn your cloud so that it is right side out.

- Press your cloud with the iron.

- Fold in the edges of your cloud's opening and then press again.

- Stitch around your cloud a little bit from the edge.

It is recommended that a quarter of an inch. You are now done with this project and can give your cute little clouds to someone you care about and brighten their day. The neat thing about this project is that it is able to go with any shape you wish. You could have so much fun with this by making rainbows, dinosaurs, flags, and military camo. The options are endless, and you can gain great ideas for fabrics and materials to do this project with. It is also a good beginner's project to do because you can get used to different commands on the machine as well.

4.5 Cosmetic Bag Designed with Cricut

Supplies Needed

- Fabric for the outside

- Thread

- 9-inch zipper Lining fabric

- Bags bottom fabric

- Cosmetic bag pattern Cricut Cutting Mat

Instructions

- Open your pattern up and cut out the pieces that you will need to make the cosmetic bag. While you are doing this, cut the lining that you will need also.

- Using the mat, cut the outer fabric and then the inner fabric. Use the 'Cotton' setting for the lining.

- Cut the bag's bottom with sturdy material and choose whichever setting matches the fabric used.

- If you use the Cricut faux leather, you will have a sturdy bottom that does not cost as much as real leather but is just as sturdy.

- Place the right sides together and proceed to sew one of the outside panels to the pieces that are used for the bottom. This should leave a 1/8-inch allowance for the seam. This should be the measurement for all seams.

- Repeat this step with the lining and the bottom.

- Next, place your zipper face down with the right side of the zipper on the outside of the bag. Then, place the top edge of the lining at the top of the zipper, lying face down. Line your edges perfectly and pin them together.

- Using a zipper foot that is attached to your sewing machine, sew the zipper close to the teeth. At the end of the pull, stop and place the needle down into the material. Lift your sewing foot up and pull your zipper from the machine past the point that is already sewn. Place the foot back down and continue sewing.

- Iron this fabric so that it is smooth, and then sew a top stitch on the edge of the fabric. Repeat this step on the other side. Place the outside of the fabric lying face up, and then place the lining face down. Pin these pieces together with your zipper foot, following the same steps you did previously. Iron this side and then proceed to finish the top stitch.

- Sew your other outside bottom piece and then sew the sides of the lining to the bottom of the lining. Make sure to leave the opening about a few inches wide so you are able to turn it inside out later on. Making sure you have the zipper open, proceed to sew the edges of the bag together. This should be the lining end to the bottom of your bag.

- Proceed to sew the corners and then flatten the unseen edges and center your seams. Sew the piece closed and then repeat the process for the bottom as well as the lining.

- Trim up all your hanging threads and the parts of the zipper that are sticking past the edge of your fabric bag. Using the unsewn hole flip the bag right side out and check your work.

- Sew up your lining hole by folding the raw edge just a bit, making sure to sew close to the edge.

- Backstitch to make sure the sewing is permanent and trim the ends off. Push your lining into the bag and push your corners out of the bag to properly form the bag. Zip your zipper and admire your work

4.6 Fabric Bookmark Made Using a Cricut

Supplies Needed

- Using a Design Space file that is designated for the bookmark's size, cut the fabric.

Instructions

- Start with placing the fabric on the cutting mat and running it through the Cricut with the appropriate settings. If you are making more than one bookmark, then copy the bookmark onto the Design Space within the parameters of the cutting mat.

- You will need pieces of fabric per bookmark.

- Using a Cricut Maker, you are able to cut more pieces at a faster pace.

- Cut your interfacing fabric or cardboard into the dimensions of 6.75" h x 0.75" w, with one per bookmark.

- Attach your fabrics together with the wrong sides facing using some pins. Sew your long sides and the bottom together. Use your foot that is for edgestitch to guide the fabric with a straight line. Sew with the needle down setting in order to pivot at the end of the corners. Make sure you backstitch the beginnings and ends of the lines.

- Fold the casing of your bookmark on the right side. Using a pencil, you can push the corners of the bookmark out so that it is right side out. Using your iron, press the casing to flatten.

- Insert the interfacing fabric that is fusible inside your bookmark.

- Fold over the top edge and use the iron to press it with heat.

- Proceed to sew the top shut.

- Using the iron, press the bookmark so that it is fused and flat. The heat will fuse the bookmark and interfacing fabric. Now that you are done, you will be able to make bookmarks out of fabric.

4.7 Leather Geometric Buffalo Pillow

Supplies Needed

- Cricut Maker Cricut X Cardstock Cricut Cutting

- Mat Cricut Fine Point Blade

- Glue or Tape Runner

Instructions

- Use the connection above to resize the flowers to the size you need, then click 'Make It.'

- Once cut, you can collect any parts you want. I hotly attached my toothpicks to the top of my cake. For the term topper, I used bigger wood skewers to stand above the flowers. Instead of flowers, this would be super sweet with mini paper rosettes. Use paper and your Cricut maker to create custom cake decor. With every addition to the tools the maker utilizes, the Cricut Maker has already made it so much easier to create the possibilities.

4.8 Fabric Wreath with Flowers

Supplies Needed

- A ring from an old lampshade
- Ribbon to wrap the lampshade
- Cricut Maker
- Cricut felt in various colors
- Rotary blade Cricut x mat for fabric
- Hot glue gun and sticks of glue
- Felt balls Wreath forms Colors that I used for my flowers are:
- White, Mauve, Olive green, Marigold, Salmon, Charcoal, Peach, Blue, Pink, Dusty Blue, Pale green

Instructions

- To use your Cricut Design Space, you need to log in.
- In the Cricut Design Space, you will need to click on 'New Project' and then select the image that you would like to use for your flowers. You can use the search bar on the right-hand side at the top to locate the image that you wish to use.
- Next, click on the image and click 'Insert Image' so that the image is selected.
- Click on each one of the files that are in the image file and click the button that says 'Flatten' at the lower right section of the

screen. This will turn the individual pieces into one whole piece. This prevents the cut file from being individual pieces for the image.

- Now, you want to resize the image so that it is the size that you wish it to be. This can be any size that is within the recommended space for the size of the canvas.

- If you want duplicates of the image for a sheet of flowers, then you should 'Select All' and then edit the image, and click 'Copy.' This will allow you to copy the whole row that you have selected.

- Once you have copied, you can then edit and paste the multiple images to make a sheet. This is the easiest way to copy and paste the image over and over again.

- Using the project that is listed in the Cricut manual, you can find the directions for the flowers. Once the flowers are cut out, you can begin to place them together with the instructions that are listed below.

- Using each one of the succulents, place the tabs together using glue. Secure your leaves together. Repeat each piece until they are done. Stack them together to create a succulent.

- Use the hot glue and place the smaller circle in the center of the finished ones. Each flower should be stacked three pieces tall with a small dot in the center.

- The Dahlia should be put together like this: Once you have cut the flowers out, you can begin to glue the pieces together.

- Start by folding the 8 tabs into the petals and gluing them down.

- Repeat this step with each piece. Stack them together so that each petal is offset. Once you have stacked your pieces, you are able to use rolled pieces or a felt ball.

- Felt peonies can be put together like this: Using glue, place the 6-tab pieces on each one of the petals. Then, proceed to stack them, making sure to use the 0 petal ones first.

- Offset each petal section so that it is not laying on top of each other in order. Finish it all off with a ball that is rolled into the center.

- Poppies can be by following these instructions: Glue the poppy tabs to each other to secure the petals. Repeat each piece of petal together to create the second poppy. Lay them together in a staggered form. Finish the flower off with a rolled center or ball made of felt.

- After the flowers and the succulents are assembled, you can begin to arrange them all over the ring covered in ribbon. Using glue, place the flowers in the order that you want to cover the ring or in a decorative fashion.

4.9 Sugar Skulls with the Cricut

Supplies Needed

- Printer Toothpicks

- Standard cardstock x standard

- grip mat for Cricut Sugar skull 'Print then Cut' image

- Cricut Explore machine

- Cricut Design Space software

- Glue

Instructions

- To use your Cricut Design Space, you need to log in.

- In the Cricut Design Space, you will need to click on 'New Project' and then select the image that you would like to use for your sugar skulls. You can use the search bar on the right-hand side at the top to locate the image that you wish to use.

- Next, click on the image, and click 'Insert Image' so that the image is selected.

- Click on each one of the files that are in the image file and click the button that says 'Flatten' at the lower right section of the screen. This will turn the individual pieces into one whole piece. This prevents the cut file from being individual pieces for the image.

- Now, you want to resize the image so that it is the size that you wish it to be. This can be any size that is within the recommended space for the size of the canvas.

- If you want duplicates of the image for the sheet of sugar skulls, then you should 'Select All' and then edit the image, and click 'Copy.' This will allow you to copy the whole row that you have selected. Once you have copied, you can then edit and paste the multiple images to make a sheet. This is the easiest way to copy and paste the image over and over again.

- Follow the instructions that are on the screen for printing, then cut the sugar skull images.

- Using glue, piece the front and back of the sugar skull together to create the topper with the toothpick inserted into the center of the pieces.

4.10 Pendant with Monogram

Supplies Needed

- Necklace chain
- Jewelry pliers
- Cricut gold pen
- Cricut Explore
- Air Cricut strong mat grip
- Cricut faux leather
- Jump ring
- Fabric fusion

Instructions

- Start by opening the Cricut Design Space. Choose the size that you want the pendant to be. This can be a circle pendant. Using the machine, make another circular-sized pendant.

- Attach the jump ring here later after the circles have been made.

- Next, open the text section in the Design shop, and type in the exact initials that you would like to use.

- Select the section that has a 'writing style' option from the menu and adjust the font of the lettering to whatever you wish.

- Drag your letter to the center part of the circle and resize it to fit the appropriate size.

- Be sure to make a front and a back. This will ensure both sides of the piece look like leather.

- Create your circle so that it matches the other one minus the letter.

- Make this an attached set.

- Using the Cricut pen, begin to cut the pieces. As it is cutting the leather, it will print the initials.

- Use your fabric fusion glue to join the two pieces of leather together, making the pendant.

- Using the pliers for jewelry, you can twist on the ring for the necklace.

- Attach your pendant and jump ring together, and then string them onto the chain.

- The pliers can close the jump ring.

4.11 DIY Leather Headphones Keeper

With leather (or fake leather), you can create so many fun items! Bracelets, earrings, keychains, wallets, journals, and much more!

Your headphones are kept knot-free by the little cord-keepers, and they are super adorable too! Offer them as presents (they make a perfect gift for a hard-to-buy-for teen), create one for yourselves, and hold the hassle of twisted cords at bay!

Machine

Cricut Explorer or Cricut Maker

Supplies Needed

- Brayer tool

- Snaps with an extra-long post if using leather, or regular length for using faux leather

- Snap press

- Deep-point Blade

- Snap hole tool

- Headphones Keeper cut file Cricut leather or faux leather in your favorite color

- Strong Grip cutting mat

Instructions

- Log into the Cricut Modeling Room and upload a cut file for the Headphones Keeper.

- After tapping on the design, then using either the arrow that resides in the lower right-hand corner of the design or the Sizing option in the upper toolbar, scale the design to 6.5 inches in length. Please press Make It. Set the sort of leather you're using for your cutting stuff. Through your Cricut, mount your deep-point blade. Place the polished side of the leather flat on your cutting mat. To drive the leather back onto the mat, use the brayer stone by using the arrow on the right-hand side of the Cricut to load your slicing mat into your Cricut.

- Look for the Cricut C to begin blinking. Once your mat is loaded, click the trigger, and your computer will start cutting. Once your machine has done cutting, make sure that your template has sliced all the way through before using the arrow to unload the mat.

- To make the Cricut repeat the cut, click the Cricut C if it hasn't. When your computer completes cutting, and you are happy that all the way through your template is sliced, click the arrow again, and it will unload your mat.

- Peel off the cutting mat with your leather pattern. Three corners of the triangle fold in. To punch a hole wherever your snap heads are, use your snap hole tool and then apply snaps to the headphone keeper with your snap click. Hold inside the ear keeper with your headphones, and embrace tangle-free headphones

4.12 DIY Create a Journal Cover

In this venture, we're using fake leather with wood grain, but you might use standard leather as well. We are going to add an HTV decal to the front that says, "Create a Beautiful Life" to give this leather a beautiful, one-of-a-kind look. You might also keep the front of the cover blank, use a quotation of your own, and even insert a logo! Play about with various fake leather or leather colors and finishes to give this Journal an appearance that's also 100 % perfect, as special as you are!

Machine

Cricut Explore or Cricut Maker Project

Supplies Needed

- Coordinating thread Easy Press or iron
- Easy Press Mat or a towel to protect your work surface
- Regular grip-cutting mat
- Fine-point blade
- Sewing machine Journal Cover and Create a Beautiful Life cut files
- Two pieces of Cricut faux leather in your favorite color and finish (we used a wood grain faux leather)
- HTV in your favorite color Weeding tools Wonder clips or bulldog clips

Instructions

- Sign in, upload the Journal Cover, and Build a Gorgeous Life cut files to Cricut Design Space. Tap on and scale each journal item. You'll like to estimate the width of the Journal for the huge chunk, twice it, and attach 1 inch. You would want to weigh the height of your Journal and add 1 inch to it for the height. Adjust the height for the two small bits because they're the same height as the main cover piece of the book. We wanted to use one color from outside the Journal for our project and a second color for the inside flaps.
- Please press Make It. Set the sort of faux leather you're using for your cutting stuff. On your cutting mat, lie your imitation

leather using the arrow on the right-hand side of the Cricut to bring your cutting mat into your Cricut. Wait for the Cricut C to begin blinking when your mat is mounted, click the button, and your machine will start to cut. If Cricut has stopped cutting, press the arrow button again to unload the mat. Cut the iron-on on the pad with the colored hand facing down. Use the mirror slider mostly on the cutting board on the left side of the screen to set the Cricut iron-on when cutting and mirroring your pattern.

- With the completed side facing down, place your long strip of faux leather on your worktop. With the polished side facing up, place the two smaller bits of faux leather on top of the large piece. On the right, line up one part, and on the left, the other piece. Clip into place.

- Use your sewing machine to stitch using a -inch seam allowance all the way across your Journal covering. Once you start stitching and again at the end, make sure to backstitch.

- Weed the iron-on, removing the area around the words, leaving the plastic backing with only the design. Don't forget to weed the letters inside as well (for example, inside the e, a, f, etc.).

- Heat the Simple Press or iron to the required temperatures for the iron-on you are using. Set your iron-on where you like it to be put on the cover of your book, using the guidelines for the sort of iron-on that you are using to click.

- Slip your Journal's front and back covers between the flaps of your journal cover.

Chapter 05: DIY Special Materials

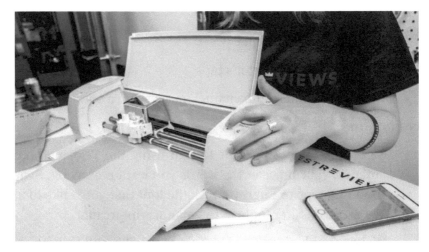

Some of the most well-known Cricut craft items are mentioned, but that's only the beginning. You'll be able to expand your creative horizons considerably with a Cricut. Brass will be engraved; In this chapter, you'll learn how to retrieve glass, spruce up your mobile phones, "go down under" with a delightful felt craft, travel through design history with some charming shrink plastic zipper handles, and ultimately, know when to use Foil Quill!

5.1 Engraved Quote Bracelet

Do you need one more excuse to join the family of Cricut Maker? The engraves it! Oh yeah, you've read it correctly! That engraves it! An inlay tip was created by Cricut, which can be used in the Cricut Creator Adaptive Tool slot! Go to your favorite art shop, check out the jewelry department, and you will be impressed by all the amazing blanks on which you can engrave dog tags, pendants, bracelets, earrings, and more! In this project. We will teach you how to build a beautiful etched quote bracelet! Select a quote, title, date, or other phrases that are important to you and engrave them. Using these very same measures in your local craft store's jewelry segment to engrave any blanks you spot!

Supplies Needed

- Cricut Engraving Tip Bracelet

- blank Bracelet bending bar

- Strong Grip cutting mat

- Masking tape or painter's tape

- Optional: Metal stamp enamel marker and a soft cloth

Instructions

- Sign in to Space at Cricut Design using the Text method to enter on your bracelet the words you want engraving. Switch from Linetype to Engrave. Pick the font that you'd like to use. We prefer to filter fonts in the manuscript format.

- Weigh the blank cuff and decide how tall it will be with your font. Use the arrow buttons that show in the corner when clicking on the words or the Sizing tool in the toolbar to size the term to the right size for your bracelet. Click on the design until your word is appropriately sized, and look for the + sign that indicates where the design's core is. Take mention of where the design's core is. When setting your bracelet on your cutting board, you can use it.

- Please press Make It. Put the bracelet on the cutting board and put it in place with tape. We want to put our jewelry on it so that it reflects on one of the lines. Pay particular attention to where the bracelet is on the cutting board, then put your word in Design Space so that it can be focused on the cutting mat where your bracelet is. Select Continue, and the Cricut Creator will be paired. Choose a sheet of aluminum as the cutting material. With the engraving tip, fill your Cricut Maker. To mount your mat, use the arrow button on your device. Now press the blinking Cricut C. Click the arrow button again to offload your mat after your Cricut has completed engraving.

- Use the bending bar of your bracelet to bend your bracelet. Optional step: use a metal stamp enamel marker to color the etched lines over the characters if you really want them to be darker. For 2 minutes, keep the paint on and then brush away with a clean, dry towel

5.2 Pop socket Covers

Mobile phone cases are so enjoyable to tailor to suit your style! With a cool pattern, you can cover your whole mobile phone case or keep it basic and cover the pop socket with a fun sticker that you can quickly alter whenever the mood hits! You can make your own pop-socket covers using your own templates and Circuit's Print and Cut feature once you know the fundamentals of this project!

Supplies Needed

- Fine-tip blade Cell phone with a pop socket
- Printable vinyl or printable sticker
- Paper Craft Tool
- Pop socket cut file
- Printer Regular grip cutting mat

Instructions

- Sign in to Space at Cricut Design. Upload the Pop socket Covers Craft Tools using the Cut File Upload guidelines for importing designs for Print and Cut.

- To calculate how broad the stickers ought to be, weigh the pop socket. Our pop socket is 1.5 inches wide, so we want each of our stickers to be just 1.5 inches shy. To get your stickers to the correct scale, click on the photo and use the measuring arrows and the Design Space calculation grid. Tip for Pro-Crafter To take up the whole page, repeat your photos, so you have extra pop socket covers for later. They're even making super cool planner stickers!

- Please press Make It by Using your printer to print your pop socket covers. Place printable vinyl or printable stickers on your content form, depending on what content you are using.

Use the arrow button on your computer to lay your printed page on the slicing mat and mount it to your Cricut. The blinking C is pressed.

- Detach the sheet from the cutting board, peel up a sticker, and put it on your pop socket until your Cricut has sliced the stickers. The Print and Cut functionality of Cricut is too much joy to use! Utilizing printable vinyl as well as the Print and Cut feature, which other projects would you consider?

5.3 DIY Etched Wine Glass

There are so many opportunities that you can do if you know how to manufacture etched glass with your Cricut, but with a little support from your Cricut, you can certainly do beautifully etched glass jobs. Stencil vinyl and etching cream are the tricks! You'll see a glass surface anywhere you look, which is just waiting to have a pattern engraved in it!

Machine

Cricut Explore or Cricut Maker Project (Cricut Joy Compatible)

Supplies Needed

- Rubber gloves
- Etching cream
- Paintbrush
- Measuring tape
- Sipping Pretty cut file
- Stencil vinyl Regular grip
- Cutting mat Fine-tip blade
- Wine glass Dish soap
- Rubbing alcohol Weeding tools
- Transfer tape Scraper tool

Instructions

- Utilizing soap and water, rinse the wine glass properly. Wipe it down with rubbing alcohol.

- Sign in to Space at Cricut Design. Attach the Sipping Pretty cut file by using Cut File Upload directions by tapping on the design and then using the up arrow in the right-hand corner or using the Sizing tool in the upper toolbar to calculate the area of your wine glass that you really want the engraved glass to cover and scale the design accordingly.

- Press the Connect button on the bottom right-hand toolbar with both parts of your template selected. Please press Make It by choosing Stencil Vinyl as your cutting material, and follow the instructions on the monitor. Place your stencil vinyl with the paper backing facing down on your cutting pad and mount it by using the arrow button on your device into your Cricut. The blinking C is pressed. Click the arrow to offload the cutting mat until the Cricut has stopped cutting.

- Remove the area outside the square and inside the heart, and leave the characters and square behind with the white paper backing, using your weeding tool to weed your vinyl. In the middle of the letters, like the inside of the p, e, y, etc., do not forget to weed.

- Substantially larger than the template cut a sheet of transfer tape. Place the transfer tape over the weeded pattern and take off the paper backing. Force the tape down onto your vinyl by dragging your remover tool over the transfer tape. Shave the transfer tape slowly, ensuring that each piece of the template lifts with the transfer tape.

- Put your transfer tape on the glass where you'd like your template. To drive the pattern down onto the mirror, use your scraper tool. Peel up the transfer tape gently, exposing the stencil vinyl. Please ensure the stencil vinyl adheres tightly to the cup. If there are some places where the vinyl does not contact the cup, it could get beneath the etching cream.

- Place on rubber gloves and obey the etching cream kit directions. Use your paintbrush to rub the etching cream gently onto the bottle, coating the region where the heart and letters are. Allow to rest for the prescribed period of time, and use water to clean off cautiously.

- Erase the vinyl stencil and see your lovely logo left behind. With that kind of venture, there are so many pleasant choices, from monogrammed wedding glasses to cups for a girl's night out to engraved glass casserole dishes & pie sheets!

Tip

For Crafter, Cautiously dry off the glass and add further etching cream. If the glass is not as engraved as you would want it to be, keep it on for the next 5 to 10 minutes, then clean again. In order to make sure our edges are smooth and clean, we also prefer to remove the heart and then hand-paint the etching cream on the glass where the heart is.

5.4 Foil Quill Fox Leather Lip Balm Holder

It is really an amazing little tool that is a relatively inexpensive addition to your Cricut cutting machine. What's a Quill Foil? The Foil Quill helps you to transform a foiling machine into your cutting machine! The Foil Quill is a tiny, pen-like device that you put into your Cricut pen holder. It has a string that your plugin, which turns hot the Foil Quill's tip. On top of the material, you intend to film, put a sheet of We R Memory Keepers foil, install it into the cutting machine, and rather than drawing the template with a pen, the Foil Quill's going to draw this with foil! What Are the Tip Sizes That Come With the Foil Quill?

Three tip sizes actually come from the Foil Quill: fine, regular, and bold. I've got the Foil Quill basic tip. Foil Materials For card-makers as well as other paper crafters, the Foil Quill is a fantasy come to fruition; you can use it on other fabrics, too! Three of our favorite foil fabrics are fake leather, cardstock, felt, and chipboard!

A Special Note on the Quill Foil Not made by Cricut, but endorsed by Cricut, is the Foil Quill. Since Cricut has not checked itself, it is a third-party attachment. The use of a Foil Quill in your system could void your warranty of Memory We R. On their webpage, Keepers has a note stating that if you run into any warranty problems with your Cricut as a result of the Foil Quill, you can contact them. You are designing a faux leather lip balm holder for this project that can be used with a sweet saying, your name, initials, or even a pattern by Foil Quill. It is recommended to go up and say Pucker. These holders of lip balm will make perfect stocking stuffers and present for Valentine's Day. Add it to your keys, bag, or pocket, and it will still be within sight of your lip balm! What are you going to think about putting yours on?

Machine

- Cricut Explore or Cricut Maker Project

Supplies Needed

- Sewing machine Thread in coordinating colors
- Scissors
- Regular grip-cutting mat
- Faux leather
- We R Memory Keepers Foil Sheet
- Lip Balm Holder
- cut file
- Washi tape
- We R Memory Keepers
- Foil
- Quill Fine-tip blade Keyring or carabineer

- Pins or wonder clips

Instructions

- Before use, the We R Memory Wardens Foil Quill must preheat for 5 minutes. For four different types of devices, the Foil Quill comes with connectors. Choosing the connector that fits with the Cricut is the first thing you'll like to do. It is labeled with a C; slide it and tighten it on the Foil Quill until it is closed to the fingertip. Second, you'll like to pop the Cricut out of the pen adaptor. Within your Cricut, your pen adaptor is mounted, and you might not even recognize it's there! Swing below the pen holder to detach it, then press up tightly but softly. It will pop up the adaptor, and you can take it out. You should supplement your Foil Quill tool that now your pen keeper is blank. To secure it in place, put it interested in the carrier but instead close the Cricut Immobilizer. Second, you also want Foil Quill to be plugged in. The cable is not very long, so you'll actually want to get an extension cord with a USB adapter attachment pretty close by. You can also insert it into your laptop or the USB adaptor on the side of the machine if you're using a Cricut Builder. Light can shine on your foil quill until it's plugged in. A protective metal plate comes with the Foil Quill. Place it under the tip of your Foil Quill and allow it to heat up for five minutes.

- Sign in to Cricut Design Space while your Foil Quill is heating and upload the Lip Balm Holder cut file following the Cut File Upload directions

- Scale the cut file so that it is 8 inches long for conventional lip balm. Need to be using either the arrow button in the bottom right or the Scale tool in the top toolbar by tapping on the design.

- Now it's time for your lip balm holder to determine if you would like to foil it. Tap on the text box on the left-hand side of your screen until you settle on the text. Fill in the foil you like, then press the Font box. Then we press the Filter button and choose a single-layer font with a handwriting theme. Adjust the line style to Draw in the upper toolbar after you have chosen your font and typed the words you want to fold.

- On the tiny rectangular piece of your lip balm holder, put your text where you like it. Under the Alignment tool, you may wish to use the Middle press. Pick both the rectangle and the paragraph, and then press Connect until you have the text where you want it. It will allow your Foil Quill to draw your design on the rectangular piece where you like it.

- Please press Make It. On top of your slicing mat, lay your fake leather and smooth it down tightly. Grab a slice of We R Memory Keepers Foil and put it on your cutting mat, where it will be foiled by your computer. Using washi tape, tape it in place. Attach the Cricut to the Space Design and pick the type of material you are cutting. By clicking the arrow button, remove the protective metal layer from under the Foil Quill and load the cutting mat into the Cricut. Press Flickering C, and the foiling of your device will begin. Click the pause button when the foiling is finished, remove the foil from your job, and press the pause button again, and your device begins cutting. Click the arrow button to offload your mat when your device is finished cutting.

- From your slicing pad, remove your cut bits of faux leather. Place your key ring over a big piece of your lip balm holder. Fold the board in half so that all the sides are lined up, and in the narrow circle, the keyring lies. On the extreme side, from where your keyring is, line up the rectangular piece of your faux leather with the big piece. Miracle snap or pin in place of all the parts lined up.

- Using an inch seam allowance, use your sewing machine to stitch all the way from around the corners of your lip balm holder. Sew straight from across the end of the track when you get to the loop area, and then finish stitching along the fake leather side. At the start and end, do not hesitate to backstitch. Trim the extra thread with your scissors

BONUS FOR YOU - Problems & Tips

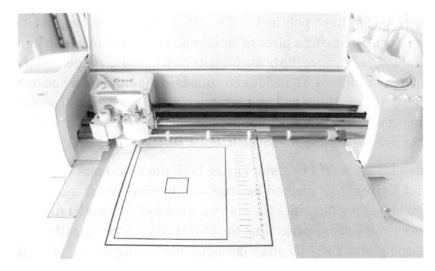

The Cricut cutting device is a fantastic invention that allows us to create a wide variety of beautiful items, but sometimes the cuts aren't as flawless as we'd like, and we're not sure why or what to do about it. Here are some things to keep in mind when using your Cricut Explore as well as Cricut Builder cutter. You'll be able to produce perfect, neat cuts with your Cricut with the help of this. You should pay attention to your Matting, Blades, Substance, Mode, and Design. In that order, namely, we address a cutting problem and then proceed with the previous steps.

The Adhesive Mat

If your Cricut mat isn't sticky enough, you won't obtain clean cuts, and if that's the case, the first thing you can do is try a different mat.

Whenever we're having problems, we just switch to a new or improved mat. If you can't afford a good mat, you might try washing it with dish detergent and letting it air dry to increase its stickiness, but we'll be honest: it may not be sticky enough even then.

In this case, a green sticky mat is preferable over a blue one. However, we seldom use the purple Firm Grip mats unless we're chopping something really thick.

The Importance of Having Clean, Sharp Blades

The blade has to be polished and spotless. All of them are great, but our favorite is having a piece of aluminum foil and rolling it up into a ball. Next, we remove the blade from its own housing, tighten the drill bit, then slowly rotate it inside and outside of the aluminum ball thirty or forty times. There will be no more bits of paper as well as vinyl clinging to your blade since our product removes them along with any other residue. (It doesn't polish it, but it performs its job.)

This strategy is effective when using both the Fine-Point and Deep-Point Knives. This method has been really effective for us. We still need knives for this since the cuts we want to make are so intricate. However, if you're worried that the blade is slicing too far rather than returning straight, you may be using the wrong blade. Only the Professional Fine-Point (German Graphite) blade may be used with Cricut Explore or Cricut Creator. The WHITE and RED caps on the Superior Fine-Point Blades packaging might be used to identify them. The grey cap cutters are obsolete since they were made for earlier models of Cricut machines, and also, the Cricut Explores and Builders are too short to be practical.

Quality Materials

Your material will also have a significant impact on the way it is sliced. For example, not all papers are created equal. More tearing may occur if the material's fibers are weak or short, as is often the case with lower-grade paper. As a result, if the paper still doesn't seem to cut correctly even after using a sticky mat and a cleaned razor, the paper could be to blame. Several times, we had an obstacle, but after switching to a new document, everything was resolved successfully. Like Recollections paper, Cricut paper is of the highest quality.

A Review of Your Preferences

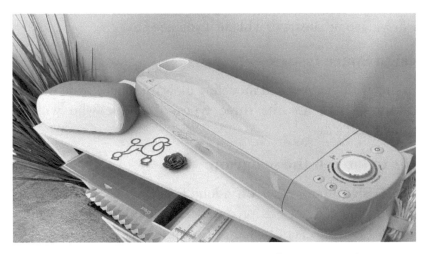

The correct configuration of the material is of paramount importance. We found that it was more convenient to display the product settings inside Cricut Design Space than on the Cricut dial. If you have a Cricut Explore, all you have to do is set the dial to Custom, and then you'll be prompted to choose your material before it's sliced.

(Please be aware that you are now operating under "customer settings" since the Manufacturer seems to have no such dial.) Add more force to the cut if it doesn't accomplish the trick. For sophisticated vinyl cuts, it might be helpful to think of your configuration choices as "Washi Cassette," even if they technically aren't.

Examine the Structure

To say nothing of the fact that not all forms will be precisely defined. They would be more difficult to cut in half if they were larger, more intricate, or both. Sometimes they are just insufficient. Still, if that's your only option, you may want to think about making them larger. If it doesn't work, or if you don't have any other options, you may try switching the content to Complicated Cuts if you're cutting paper or the washi paper setting if you're cutting vinyl. None of them are likely to work, but it can't hurt to give them a go.

As a result of their size or complexity, certain patterns cannot be cut cleanly. Nothing is really lost, so you can always go back and trim it down with some shears or a blade if you need to.

Design Space Issues

Working with pictures and modeling tools presents a wide variety of difficulties. Here are the three types of people who will need technological aid:

Fails to launch the program

Cricut Design Room relies on Adobe Flash, so be sure you have it installed. You can get this program from Adobe's website, and it's free. Most web browsers, including Chrome, will ask you the first time you access Design Room whether you want to enable Flash to run. In order to utilize the app, you must touch the Enable button.

Cannot Locate Photographic Materials

If you want to use the preset files, you'll have to unzip the package first. There are unzip systems available for free, or you may have previously created one. Once your files have been uploaded, the formatting window must be visible. If it doesn't, go to the appropriate folders in Template Space and click the "insert pictures" button. A green check mark has to be next to these if you are unsure of what sort they are.

We Get a Bad Vibe From Imported Images.

Seeing gaps or just one color in the photo after you've uploaded it is more indicative of an issue with the texturing. Select everything in your template with a single click of Ctrl+A, and then make the fill color stand out by choosing something more fitting. You've figured out that there's a hidden layer inside you that's causing all of these problems. Presently you are able to see through it, and you may go ahead and finish editing.

Similar to other systems, Design Space might provide challenges even before you begin using it. Once you've progressed to a higher level and are eager to unlock further features, any issues you encounter will be trivial to fix.

BONUS FOR YOU - Making Money with Cricut

It's possible that your innovative ideas and newly acquired abilities will play a role in the company's design and development. Enthusiastic beginners could run across problems like

The Initial Phase

As with any new venture, answering the big questions is essential for overcoming obstacles. As an example, it is essential to discuss issues like identifying our target market, determining the most appropriate products to provide, identifying alternative channels for expanding our reach and establishing a sustainable profit margin from the outset. To put it another way, you'll need to start with a company plan that's tried and true.

The Scope of the Business

You need to find a way to sell your products that is different from anybody else's, whether that means breaking into the international market physically or virtually. To increase sales as effectively as possible, it is preferable to focus efforts on a single strategy.

Keep in mind that your ultimate goal should be to maximize profit and use that money to grow your business. As a result, increasing profits increases the likelihood of investing in cutting-edge methods and materials, leading to better productivity. You may measure your success using your company concept.

Methods of Actual Sector Infiltration

You'll look at the potential of sending things from business to business. The methodology places equal value on the total number of acquisitions and transactions. The most difficult part of starting a new Cricut-based company is increasing production volume.

Having committed job assurances allows you to bargain for a fair amount with vendors, which is a huge benefit. Similarly, it is difficult to find such shining chances since such contracts are susceptible to market pressures. As a new firm, you are free to market your wares only to commercial clients. While businesses always seek novel ideas and high-quality materials, they might benefit from a concept of working time.

The goal of establishing such a link is to make the industry a jumping-off point for more relationships, which would lead to more upselling possibilities. It's not easy to get a part since the competition is so fierce.

Sales from "business to customer" might be seen as an alternative to "memory" sales. The goal of this method is to offer your goods to retail consumers who are interested in acquiring them.

Thus, the number of sales is taken into account. The success of your business might be attributed to your creative thinking, new ideas, or the medium and approach you choose to use (T-shirts, mugs, etc.).

Locating a suitable retail location to showcase your wares is crucial. One of the goals of a new start project is to see a variety of locations and objects.

In comparison to the other methods discussed, the kick expense is little, which is good news for consumers. However, starting a new company from scratch is never easy.

The first stage would include word-of-mouth as well as producing high-quality products at reasonable costs.

Regard and Tidy Up

Over time and with continued usage, dust or paper fragments may accumulate in your machine, and you may notice that oils from your machine are accumulating along the carriage's path. Easy cleanup is guaranteed!

Here are some suggestions to keep in mind while cleaning your Explore device:

- If you need to clean your gadget, remember to always disconnect it first.

- The machine housing may be wiped down with a dampened paper towel and some cleaning agent.

- If you see dust with paper particles accumulating due to static electricity, you may remove them entirely by wiping the affected area with a dry cloth.

- If you see grime building up on the rail the train travels along, you may gently wipe it away with a tissue, swab, or clean cloth.

Important

The plastic covering of the machine will be severely damaged by acetone, even if it's in a nail polish remover.

How to Apply Grease

As a first step, you should power off the Cricut Explore device. Second, push the cut smart carriage's left button lightly to move it. Third, wipe the cut clever carriage bar (the bar the carriage travels on, immediately in front of the belt) with a cotton swab to clean it. The clever cut carriage is pushed by a gentle rightward motion. Turn the cut smart trolley bar around and wipe it off with a tissue in the other direction. Slowly begin bringing the clever cut carriage toward the middle of the machine. Remove the lid from the lubricant container and apply a little bit to the tip of the cotton swab. A clever-cut carriage may be made smoother by greasing the area surrounding the bar on both ends of the carriage.

Chapter 06: Troubleshooting Techniques

Designs are stored online, so which you may choose a design and make changes to it using a device, laptop, or smartphone phone, depending on your preference. The Cricut Picture Collection is an enormous resource since it has over 50,000 different photographs, projects, and fonts from which you may choose or to which you can contribute your own designs.

6.1 Inability to Locate the Knife

If your Cricut machine is giving you trouble because the blade isn't being detected, try the solutions given below.

- Before proceeding to the Attach Tools phase, check that the tool currently installed in Clamp B is compatible with the tool recommended by Design Space upon that project's main screen. If the selected approach is not available, you may switch tools by unloading the pad and going to the project to establish the overall from there. If the issue persists after the proper tool is attached, go to step two.

- Second, release the tool and gently wipe off the housing's shining surface on clamp B. You should now reconnect the tool to clamp B and press the flashing "go" button. If you are still having issues, you should go to step 3. Free the instrument from clamp B. Please clean the tip detector using an air pump or a microfiber cloth. To continue, reconnect the tool to clamp B and press the pulsating go button. Proceed to Step 4 if the issue persists. If you have access to a rotary blade, sheave, or grading Wheel, try using it for a little test project.

- With any of the options below, you may let member care know that the original unit's motor enclosure is a potential problem in the event that the trial project is successful. If the issue persists across a wide range of measurement tools, including your fingers, go on to step 5.

- Space Design, Fifth Stage Uninstall. To start fresh, uninstall Cricut Machine and reinstall it. If it doesn't work, uninstall Design Space and reinstall it. If the problem persists, you should get in touch with member services.

6.2 A red blinking light next to the power button

Determine when the red light on the power button begins blinking or flashing, and then choose the appropriate troubleshooting steps below. Whenever the PC boots up, When initially turning on the system, if the physical buttons light flash or blinks red, please contact group care through one of the ways listed below for assistance. With regards to software revisions: In the event that your device's power button indicator is blinking or lighting red when updating its firmware, please contact member care using one of the options provided below.

The following will occur when the mat is being overfilled

If the power button light remains red while you are trying to put the chopping mat into your machine, proceed as described below. Is this a common issue with several tasks in the project? If just one design is affected, it's possible that an accident occurred, in which case the design will need to be recreated. If this issue occurs across many projects, go on to step 2. Any debris or dust on the roller bars might have been the cause of the blunder. Once the dust has settled, turn off the machine and run the carriage car over the slider bar three or four times. Please be free to reach out to customer care for more assistance if this doesn't help.

This will occur if the mat, blade, or material becomes entangled in the material.

Does this happen with any kind of substance? If it happens, there might be issues with the gadget. First, turn the machine off (or unplug it) and move the cradle vehicle back and forward between six times. Then, reconnect the machine and attempt the design again.

When you need assistance, don't hesitate to contact our friendly Member Support team. What part of the knife are you employing? The steel blade of the knife is tempered to easily slice through tough materials like leather, even balsa wood. A red flashing light indicates that the blade has been stuck in thicker material, which is to be expected. In order to resume the cut, just follow the on-screen instructions, clear the area, and press the cut button again.

This often happens many times throughout a cut. Please be free to reach out to member assistance for more assistance if this doesn't help.

6.3 Tool Is either Dragging or Tearing

There are a number of possible events that might cause the machine to tear the material. The good news is that this problem is usually easy to repair when a few basic troubleshooting steps are taken.

Things to think about if the Cricut Exploration or Cricut Maker equipment is struggling to cut through the material:

- Be careful to use the Design Space or the smart set dial to choose the appropriate material configuration.

- If you decide to go with a custom setup, be sure to choose the appropriate material from the drop-down selection.

- Verify the scope and depth of the image. If you're having trouble cutting an image that's very detailed or thin, try cutting one that's simpler or bigger.

- If the issue is resolved while cutting a basic image, try the Cardstock custom option, which makes very precise cuts.

- If you have a Craft Knife or Cricut Machine Air 2 and you are having trouble cutting, consider turning off Fast Mode and cutting again.

- When you've detached the blades from the unit's housing, check within the blade's framework and on the blade itself for dust.

- Reduce pressure by a factor of 2–4 for that material type in the management custom materials screen. To modify the custom materials used in the Mat Preview, tap the Adjust Content button and then either go to the profile's control custom components screen or click the edit custom materials button on the top middle of the Mat Preview window.

This procedure may need to be repeated a couple of times until the desired cut is achieved. An ideal setting for cutting copy paper would be a dedicated cutting area. Maybe the material you're trying to cut isn't ideal for lasers. Use a clean blade and a mat if at all possible. Both of these things may make it difficult to heal wounds.

Please feel free to contact helping clients for further assistance if the issue persists after trying the above solutions.

6.4 Weird Noise Coming From the Machine

No one appreciates a device that makes constant noise. If your Cricut machine is making an unusual sound, try the steps in the troubleshooting section. Fractionalization of Sound: If you hear a strange grinding noise coming from your Cricut Maker or Explore, try the following:

If the carriage vehicle makes a loud noise when you push the cut button, as if it were hitting the unit's surface, please capture a brief short video of the issue and contact Member Services. The agent may suggest sending a reference file or video so that a professional may have a look at the issue. Please contact member support if the first time you use a new gadget results in an unusual sound. If you've solved the new cutting difficulty before by using the tool efficiently, go on to step 3. Thirdly, always use the device's original power cord. If you're utilizing a certain brand or configuration, the voltage may be off, causing a grinding noise.

If you are using the supplied power cable, please proceed to step 4. You are probably using a force that is too great. To lower the previously assigned object, you are attempting to cut by 2–4, pick "modify custom materials" from the account's toolbar or select "change material" from the right-hand side of the cut preview. You'll need to repeat the process thrice before you see any change. Get in touch with our membership support team for more assistance if the issue persists after trying the above.

Noise level

To find out why your Creator or Explore Air 2 could be quieter than normal when cutting or writing, you can switch to quick mode. This option is selected on the make page in the design room. You should record the audio issue and send it to member support if the quick mode is not involved.

6.5 Can't Get the Cricut to Cut

If the Cricut Explore machine isn't cutting all the way throughout your material or is just scoring the surface, the issue may usually be fixed by doing some basic troubleshooting. Here are some steps to try:

- When using a gadget mat in Design Space and any smart set's dial, verify that the selected environment setting is appropriate for the material.

- If you have set the Cricut Explore to custom mode, double-check that you have selected the suitable materials from the customized materials list.

- Release the blade housing by opening clamp B. Make sure a blade made by Cricut is being utilized.

- The next step is to check the blade and its housing, removing any dust that may have been lodged in the housing. Make a test slice once you've cleaned up. If it didn't get the knife blade housing clean, go on to step 3.

- Raise the stress by 2–4 for chosen material reality using the Profile menu's Manage custom materials option, and then cut a sample. Depending on the material being cut, you may need to adjust the pressure settings anywhere from two to three times at intervals of two to four.

- Try slicing a material like a scrap paper at the right setting for that article.

- Think we'll arrive at the same conclusion? If not, it will be difficult to make the necessary cuts in the raw material.

- Fifth, delete any temporary internet files in your browser and retry the test.

- If you're still having issues after using a different browser, try switching to Mozilla Firefox or Google Chrome.

If you've already tried steps 1–5 and the issue persists, Member Support is ready to assist you further.

6.6 Accidentally Pair Your Bluetooth Device With Another Device

Look at the steps required to forget a Bluetooth connection (Cricut Maker, for example) permanently. In this section, we'll go through how to initiate exploration) using Windows.

- First, choose Settings from the Start menu.

- Tools with several selections

- Simply choose the app or program you want to delete, click "Remove Device," and the action will be confirmed.

Please be aware that the specific steps may vary significantly depending on the OS version you're using. In order to utilize a Bluetooth device after erasing or forgetting it, you may need to repeat the pairing process.

Chapter 07: Uploading Images Into Design Space

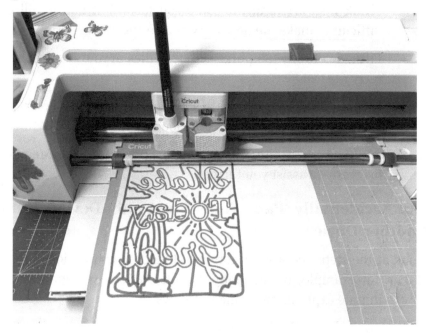

Using Design Space, you may freely import your own photographs and transform them into cut-out patterns or shapes. There are two types of image file formats that may be uploaded: basic and vector.

7.1 Typical Illustrations

Bitmap graphics and pictures (.jpg,.gif,.png, and .bmp) are included. Images are uploaded in a thin layer, and modification is available at any point throughout the process of uploading them. These are also examples of what are known as raster images.

7.2 Vector Illustrations

Provide dxf and svg file types. These files are imported according to the settings you provided during import and will be subsequently layered.

Select a device from the list below to get detailed instructions for sharing vectors and elementary pictures.

7.3 Windows/Mac

To begin adding images, choose upload on the design panel's canvas' left side. When you click the button, a window will go up where you may choose an image or pattern to upload. You may upload photos in a variety of formats, from bitmaps (jpg, gif, png, and bmp) to vector graphics (dxf, svg), with ease. To get going, click the Upload Image button. Open the file selection by clicking the browse button to locate the image you like to show on your computer or by dragging and dropping the file into the upload pane. It will follow the standard photo upload procedure if you choose a gif, jpg, bmp, or png file. The Vector image upload wizard will lead you through the process if you choose either dxf or svg as your file types.

7.4 One Possible Approach: The Bare Minimum Upload

Select an image file of type (jpg, gif, png, or bmp) to upload. After that, either open it using the file selection or drag it into the Design Space picture upload box. Second, read the on-screen text and decide if the image is simple, somewhat complicated, or complex. Select "next" to proceed.

In step three, you'll determine where the image was clipped. Use the wipe & select function in your erase and crop program to remove the distracting background from your image. The never-to-be-slashed areas may be seen in the checkerboard's backdrop. The filled portions are what you'll see when you upload a picture to the design program.

Once you've selected the areas to be removed from the image, you may use the preview to see the cut lines highlighted. To return to the edit window and start erasing components of the picture until the preview matches the desired result, choose to conceal the preview. Choose to go until the image meets your requirements. Label the picture with a title and tags (if necessary) to make searching easier in the future. The file may be saved as either a print-and-cut or a cut picture, depending on your preferences. To apply the picture to the design screen, it must first be saved as a print containing all of the file's interior colors and forms before being cut out. If you choose to save the photo as a Cut, just the silhouette will be preserved as the cut route. When you're done, be sure to save your work. There will be a return to the upload window. In the gallery of uploaded photographs, the most recent addition would always be shown last. Select an image from your computer, then use the Insert Images button to add it to your presentation.

7.5 Second Choice: Providing a Vector Image

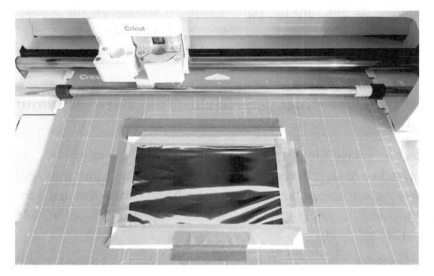

To upload a svg and dxf file to Design Space, choose it in the file selector and then click open; alternatively, you may drag the document to the image upload window.

It is important to keep in mind that Design Space may be able to read files that were produced by other design tools. You have the option of using text, illustrated layers, filled solid colors, or solid colors in the folders.

You may also utilize solid colors. If, on the other hand, a layered picture is going to be used, care must be taken to ensure that the pieces of the image are not clumped together in the first stored version of the image. Third, in order to make the process of scanning your picture simpler subsequently, give it a name and label it (if you wish to). Then, check to see that your work is being saved regularly.

After you have completed step 4, you will be sent back to the Submit page. The library would be the most recent picture contributed, and it would be located at the very bottom of the imported photographs. Simply click on the image you wish to use to choose it, and then go to the menu and select the Attach Photos option.

Conclusion

The desktop software version of Cricut Design Space is now in beta testing, and it is an online program that serves dual purposes as both a partnership application and an internet application. It grants you the capacity to produce, transport, and manage files

that are used by the Cricut Maker machine as well as the Cricut Explore machine. You have the ability to access the software on some devices over a remote connection by making use of your own personal computer, tablet, or even your mobile phone. In addition, Cricut Design Space provides you with access to a comprehensive library that is brimming with projects and other materials that can be downloaded.

We had a rather adventurous journey, but we are finally here at our destination after all that excitement. Even if this ebook has given you a lot of information on how to enhance your work on the Design Space, it is essential to keep in mind that you need to start with a tiny scale.

Even if you have a ton of crazy ideas flying through your head right now second, the best plan of action is to start working on projects that are more manageable so that you can get experience and become comfortable with the platform. This will allow you to learn more about how to use it. This in no way suggests that you need to impose limitations on yourself in any way. Simply make it a priority to develop your skills in a methodical approach so that you may reach a professional level. It is with great pleasure that I share with you at this second the news that you are no longer regarded as a newcomer to our industry.

You now have access to the vast majority of the information and knowledge that exists, and it is quite unlikely that anybody will ever take that away from you. You will, however, be required to keep up with a consistent practice routine. In the event that you go on a brief vacation, there is a possibility that you may forget about the things that are really important to you. During the time that you spend exercising, you could find that you suffer periods of moderate irritation. However, this does not mean that you should stop trying. The amount of money you invest in a Cricut is more than justified by the benefits you get from using it.

As a result, this will be the final destination of the expedition. If you have mastered all of the methods and recommendations that are mentioned in this book, then you certainly deserve some praise and congratulations. To facilitate a speedier recovery and get you back on your feet sooner, you should keep this book within easy reach until you are ready to take care of things on your own. Even when you have reached the point where you have a comprehensive knowledge of the information, you should still keep it close so that you may refer to it in the future. You might also provide this book to those in your immediate surroundings which are either new to the Design Space or are having trouble navigating the platform in their work. These individuals could benefit from having access to more information.

BONUS TIME!

Here's the tutorial I suggest about Cricut, see how it's done is always better:

There's no way I'm not suggesting the official Cricut tutorial channel, you will find a lot of playlists:

https://www.youtube.com/@Cricut/playlists

Here's some amazing playlists you will love!

https://www.youtube.com/playlist?list=PL3dzJwXFL3uIi_fVALSlEVeRRGWvMr
Cl5

https://www.youtube.com/playlist?list=PLRI7QVsVtViDgYqymWNtt5BOrumuD
Yk35

https://www.youtube.com/playlist?list=PLfa0jG_SgDO_-zKM0tIIxVNurE1zYSn2i

https://www.youtube.com/watch?v=tA8LU4S_a5I&list=PLOM6Z5mLlc4M7YpUonxPzswfpi_sV ZKiS

HOW TO DOWNLOAD NEW FILES FOR FREE AND GET BONUS CONTENT? Here's all the resources you absolutely need in your Cricut journey!

https://cricut.com//apps

https://www.creativebloq.com/features/best-free-svg-files-for-cricut

https://www.thegirlcreative.com/the-best-sites-to-download-free-svg-and-cut-files-for-cricut-and-silhouette/

And what about the best community out there? Here's the one I strongly advise, you'll find a lot of people who are starting the Cricut journey right now and experts

https://help.cricut.com/hc/en-us/articles/360027251034-How-do-I-search-for-projects-in-the-Cricut-Community-